# CONTENTS

# Introduction

WHETHER FOR HEALTH REASONS or due to ethical concerns, more and more people are rejecting animal products and turning to a vegetable-based diet and realizing that there is life after meat. With the plentiful supply of fresh vegetables, fruit, herbs, nuts, grains, pulses and pasta that is available to us, the possibilities of creating really exciting and varied recipes have never been greater.

It is not only vegetarians who can enjoy vegetarian food. The fresh, light and innovative recipes that have come to the forefront of new-style vegetarian cuisine provide a tempting departure from many of the heavier, non-vegetarian dishes. This book gathers together some of the best recipes in the world, all of them packed with fabulous tastes and textures.

You are what you eat, and we are constantly being urged to choose a diet rich in complex carbohydrates found in cereals, grains, fruits and vegetables, which are abundant in vegetarian cooking. If you include dairy products in your diet, restrict your intake by choosing skimmed or semi-skimmed milk and low-fat yogurts and cheeses. By limiting the use of oils to unsaturated types such as olive, sunflower, corn and peanut, you can reduce the level of fat in your diet considerably.

With options for everything from light snacks to special occasion dinners, every recipe here is delicious proof that eating the vegetarian way is not only nutritious, but entertaining and exciting too. Try them and enjoy them.

# Fresh Vegetables

*Thanks to the range of fresh produce now available, the choice for vegetarians has expanded enormously.*

**Asparagus**
Asparagus spears have an intense, rich flavour – delicious served with melted butter.

**Aubergines**
Differing in colour and shape, aubergines have a smoky flavour when cooked.

**Beans**
Broad beans, green beans and runner beans can be steamed or lightly boiled in salted water until *al dente*.

**Broccoli**
Quick and easy to prepare, broccoli can be eaten raw with dips, or cooked.

**Cabbage**
There are many varieties of cabbage. Care should be taken not to overcook this vegetable.

**Carrots**
Carrots have a sweet and fragrant flavour. They are just as delicious eaten raw as they are cooked.

**Cauliflower**
Cauliflower has a pleasant, fresh flavour.

**Celeriac**
Celeriac has a hint of sweet celery.

**Celery**
With its distinctive flavour, celery is an ideal ingredient for soups.

**Chillies**
Members of the capsicum family, these can be very fiery.

**Courgettes**
These are succulent and tender with a delicate flavour.

**Cucumber**
This has a crisp, refreshing taste.

**Fennel**
A crisp, delicious aniseed-flavoured vegetable.

**Garlic**
These firm, round bulbs have a very distinctive flavour.

# Index

**Leeks**

A versatile vegetable with a subtle, oniony flavour.

**Lettuce**

There are many varieties of lettuce available. Most salads include this vegetable.

**Mushrooms**

Whether cultivated or wild, mushrooms are an essential ingredient for vegetarian cooking.

**Onions**

Onions come in many different varieties. They can be sautéed, roasted or eaten raw in salads.

**Parsnips**

A sweet root vegetable with a distinct earthy flavour.

**Peas**

Sweet tender peas are unbeatable. Make the most of them when they are in season.

**Peppers**

Green peppers have a fresh "raw" flavour whereas red, yellow and orange peppers are sweeter.

**Potatoes**

Rich in carbohydrate, potatoes can be baked, boiled, fried, sautéed, mashed or roasted.

**Pumpkins/Squashes**

These have a fibrous flesh with a mild, slightly sweet flavour.

**Shallots**

These small bulbs are ideal for using in sauces.

**Spinach**

Rich in iron, spinach can be eaten raw in salads or cooked.

**Swedes**

These are ideal for adding to soups and casseroles.

**Sweetcorn**

Eaten on the cob with salt and a little butter, sweetcorn is absolutely delicious.

**Tomatoes**

These come in a variety of sizes and form the basis of many vegetarian dishes.

**Turnips**

Sweet and nutty flavoured, turnips range from very small to large, mature vegetables.

# Macaroni Soufflé

This is generally a great favourite with children, and is rather like a light and fluffy macaroni cheese. Make sure you serve the soufflé immediately after it is cooked or it will sink dramatically.

## INGREDIENTS

Serves 3–4

75g/3oz short cut macaroni

melted butter, to coat

25g/1oz/3 tbsp dried breadcrumbs

50g/2oz/4 tbsp butter

5ml/1 tsp ground paprika

40g/1½oz/⅓ cup plain flour

300ml/½ pint/1¼ cups milk

75g/3oz Cheddar or Gruyère
   cheese, grated

50g/2oz Parmesan cheese, grated

3 eggs, separated

salt and ground black pepper

1 Cook the macaroni in plenty of boiling salted water according to the instructions on the packet. Drain well and set aside. Preheat the oven to 150°C/300°F/Gas 2.

2 Brush a 1.2 litre/2 pint/5 cup soufflé dish with melted butter, then coat evenly with the breadcrumbs, shaking out any excess from the pan.

3 Put the butter, paprika, flour and milk into a saucepan and slowly bring to the boil, whisking constantly until the mixture is smooth and thick.

4 Simmer the sauce for 1 minute, then remove from the heat and stir in the cheeses until melted. Season well and mix with the cooked macaroni.

5 Beat in the egg yolks. Whisk the egg whites until they form soft peaks and spoon a quarter into the sauce mixture to lighten it slightly.

6 Using a large metal spoon, carefully fold in the rest of the egg whites and transfer to the prepared soufflé dish.

7 Bake in the centre of the oven for about 40–45 minutes until the soufflé is risen and golden brown. The middle should wobble very slightly and the soufflé should be lightly creamy inside.

# Dairy Produce

*Both local and imported dairy products are now widely available. Most have low-fat versions.*

**Butter/Margarine**
Butter is a natural dairy product made from cream. Margarine is a butter substitute made from vegetable fat.

**Buttermilk**
This is skimmed milk with an added bacterial culture, to give it a natural tangy flavour.

**Cheeses (hard and semi-hard)**
Hard cheeses are often essential for cooking and of course Parmesan is an important ingredient for many dishes.

**Cheeses (soft)**
Cottage cheese, curd cheese, mascarpone and ricotta are all soft, moist cheeses used in many dishes. Other soft cheeses of culinary note are mozzarella and tangy feta.

**Cheeses (blue)**
Blue cheeses such as gorgonzola, Roquefort and Stilton are among some of the most popular cheeses used for sauces, soups and tarts.

**Cream**
This is available in many forms including single, double, clotted, whipping, soured and crème fraîche.

**Eggs**
Rich in protein, eggs are used in both savoury dishes and desserts.

**Fromage frais**
A creamy, fresh white cheese sold in pots.

**Milk**
This is available as skimmed, semi-skimmed and full-fat, as well as condensed, powdered, homogenized and evaporated.

**Quark**
This soft white cheese is made from fermented skimmed milk.

**Yogurt**
Yogurt is available in various forms including organic, low-fat, Greek and bio.

# Autumn Glory

*Glorious pumpkin shells summon up the delights of autumn and seem too good simply to throw away. Use one instead as a serving dish. Pumpkin and pasta make marvellous partners, especially as a main course served from the baked shell.*

*Serves 4*

1.75kg/4–4½lb pumpkin
1 onion, sliced
2.5cm/1in piece fresh root ginger
45ml/3 tbsp extra virgin olive oil
1 courgette, sliced
115g/4oz sliced mushrooms
400g/14oz can chopped tomatoes
75g/3oz pasta shells
450ml/¾ pint/1¾ cups stock
60ml/4 tbsp fromage frais
30ml/2 tbsp chopped fresh basil
salt and ground black pepper

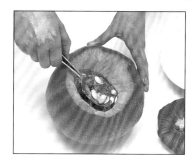

1 Preheat the oven to 180°C/350°F/Gas 4. Cut the top off the pumpkin with a large, sharp knife and scoop out and discard the pumpkin seeds.

2 Using a small sharp knife and a sturdy tablespoon, cut and scrape out as much flesh from the pumpkin shell as possible, then chop the flesh into rough chunks.

3 Bake the pumpkin with its lid on for 45 minutes–1 hour until the inside begins to soften.

4 Meanwhile, make the filling. Gently fry the onion, ginger and pumpkin flesh in the olive oil for about 10 minutes, stirring the mixture occasionally.

5 Add the sliced courgette and mushrooms and cook for a further 3 minutes, then stir in the tomatoes, pasta shells and stock. Season well, bring to the boil, then cover the pan and simmer gently for about 10 minutes.

6 Stir the fromage frais and basil into the pasta and spoon the mixture into the pumpkin. It may not be possible to fit all the filling into the pumpkin shell, so serve the rest separately if necessary.

# Pulses and Lentils

*Pulses and lentils are a good source of protein. Both need to be washed, and pulses should be soaked overnight before cooking. Beans should initially be boiled hard for ten minutes to destroy their toxins. Do not add salt until they are nearly cooked as this toughens their skins.*

### PULSES, BEANS AND SPLIT PEAS
**Black-eyed beans**
   Sometimes called black-eyed peas, these are the only beans that do not need soaking.
**Butter beans**
   These are ideal for soups or pâtés as they have a velvety texture.

**Chick-peas**
   These round, beige-coloured pulses have a strong, nutty flavour when cooked.
**Haricot beans**
   These are small, white and oval. They are ideal for slow cooking, as they absorb the flavour of herbs and spices easily.
**Kidney beans**
   Kidney beans are dark red-brown beans with quite a strong flavour.
**Green and yellow split peas**
   These tasty and nutritious peas are ideal for thick, hearty soups and are used in Indian cooking.

### LENTILS
**Brown and green lentils**
   These small lentils have a delicate flavour and retain their shape during cooking. Green lentils have a slightly stronger taste.
**Red split lentils**
   Popular and easy to cook, these lentils are often used in vegetarian dishes.
### TOFU
   This is an unfermented soya bean curd that is available in firm and silken varieties to be used in all kinds of sweet and savoury dishes as an alternative to dairy produce.

# Potato, Spinach and Pine Nut Gratin

*Pine nuts add a satisfying crunch to this gratin of wafer-thin potato slices and spinach in a creamy cheese sauce. Serve with a simple lettuce and tomato salad.*

INGREDIENTS

*Serves 2*

450 g/1 lb potatoes

1 garlic clove, crushed

3 spring onions, thinly sliced

150 ml/¼ pint/⅔ cup single cream

250 ml/8 fl oz/1 cup milk

225 g/8 oz frozen chopped spinach, defrosted

115 g/4 oz Cheddar cheese, grated

40 g/1½ oz/scant ¼ cup pine nuts

salt and freshly ground black pepper

lettuce and tomato salad, to serve

1 Peel the potatoes and cut them carefully into wafer-thin slices. Spread them out in a large, heavy-bottomed, non-stick frying pan.

2 Sprinkle the crushed garlic and sliced spring onions evenly over the potatoes.

3 Pour the cream and milk over the potatoes. Place the pan over a gentle heat, cover and cook for 8 minutes, or until the potatoes are tender.

4 Using both hands, squeeze the spinach dry. Add the spinach to the potatoes, mixing lightly. Cover the pan and cook for 2 minutes more.

5 Season with salt and pepper, then spoon the mixture into a shallow, flameproof casserole. Preheat the grill.

6 Sprinkle the grated cheese and pine nuts over the spinach mixture. Heat under the grill for 2–3 minutes until the topping begins to turn golden. Serve with a lettuce and tomato salad.

# Spices

*The inclusion of spices in a recipe can literally transform a meal.*

**Cardamom**
These pods are often used whole to add flavour to rice dishes.

**Chilli powder**
The dried seeds of chillies are ground to make a very hot and spicy powder.

**Cinnamon**
Cinnamon is available whole or ground. The sticks are used for flavour and are not eaten.

**Cloves**
Cloves are used in spice mixtures for sweet and savoury dishes.

**Coriander seeds**
These are the roasted, dried seeds of the plant.

**Cumin**
Available as whole, dark brown seeds and ground.

**Fennel seeds**
Small, light green seeds, similar in smell and taste to aniseed.

**Fenugreek seeds**
Fenugreek is used in many fish dishes and curries.

**Ginger**
Both fresh and ground ginger have a sharp, refreshing flavour. Fresh root ginger should be peeled before use.

**Mustard seeds**
Often used with vegetables and pulses, these have a nutty flavour.

**Nutmeg**
Whole or ground, nutmeg has a sweet, nutty flavour.

**Peppercorns**
Used in virtually all savoury cooking, pepper has the capacity to enhance other flavours.

**Saffron**
This expensive spice is used for its aroma and colour.

**Turmeric**
Turmeric is a bright yellow powder and is primarily used for its colouring properties.

# Cauliflower and Mushroom Gougère

*This puffy, golden-brown, cheese-flavoured case filled with lovely fresh vegetables is a wonderful dinner party dish.*

INGREDIENTS

*Serves 4–6*

115 g/4 oz/8 tbsp butter

150 g/5 oz/1¼ cups plain flour

4 eggs

115 g/4 oz Gruyère or Cheddar cheese, finely diced

5 ml/1 tsp Dijon mustard

salt and freshly ground black pepper

*For the filling*

1 small cauliflower

1 x 200 g/7 oz can tomatoes

15 ml/1 tbsp sunflower oil

15 g/½ oz/1 tbsp butter

1 onion, chopped

115 g/4 oz button mushrooms, halved if large

sprig of fresh thyme

1 Preheat the oven to 200°C/400°F/Gas 6. Butter a large ovenproof dish. Place 300 ml/ ½ pint/1¼ cups water and butter together in a large saucepan and heat until the butter has melted. Remove from the heat and add all the flour at once. Beat well with a wooden spoon for about 30 seconds, until smooth. Allow to cool slightly.

2 Beat in the eggs, one at a time, and continue beating until the mixture is thick and glossy. Stir in the cheese and mustard and season with salt and pepper. Spread the mixture around the sides of the ovenproof dish, leaving a hollow in the centre for the filling.

3 Cut the cauliflower into florets, discarding the woody, hard stalk.

4 To make the filling, purée the tomatoes in a blender or food processor and then pour into a measuring jug. Add enough water to make up to 300 ml/½ pint/1¼ cups of liquid.

5 Heat the oil and butter in a flameproof casserole. Fry the onion for 3–4 minutes. Add the mushrooms and cook for 2–3 minutes. Add the cauliflower and stir-fry for 1 minute. Add the tomato liquid and thyme. Season. Cook over low heat for 5 minutes.

6 Spoon into the hollow in the ovenproof dish. Bake for 40 minutes, until the pastry is risen.

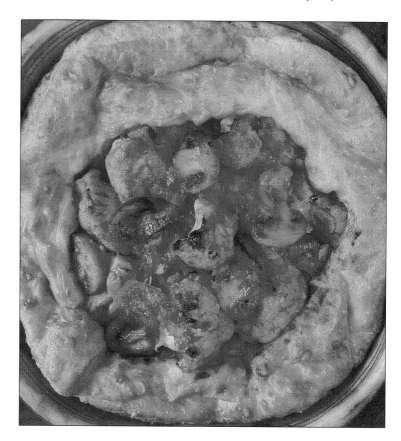

# Herbs

*Beautiful fresh herbs from around the world are readily available. This herb checklist highlights both familiar and less well-known items.*

**Basil**
Well-known for its affinity with tomatoes, basil has a spicy aroma that is a pungent mixture of cinnamon and anise.

**Bay leaves**
These are one of the oldest herbs used in cookery. When used fresh, they have a deliciously sweet flavour.

**Chives**
This herb has a very delicate oniony flavour.

**Coriander**
An intense, aromatic, sweet and spicy herb. The leaves can be used as a garnish.

**Dill**
A pungent, slightly sweet-tasting herb with anise overtones.

**Marjoram**
This is very similar to oregano, though more delicate in flavour.

**Mint**
A very versatile herb with a distinctive scent, mint is used both in sweet and savoury dishes.

**Oregano**
An aromatic and highly flavoured herb, oregano features strongly in Italian cooking.

**Parsley**
Both flat leaf and curly varieties have a slightly bitter flavour.

**Rosemary**
Rosemary, with its dark, needle-like leaves, has an intense flavour and should be used sparingly.

**Sage**
The aromatic oils in sage impart a distinct and powerful flavour.

**Savory**
With its peppery flavour, savory makes a good seasoning.

**Tarragon**
This has a sweet, aniseed flavour.

**Thyme**
A robust aromatic herb with a warm, earthy flavour.

# Celeriac and Blue Cheese Roulade

*Celeriac adds a delicate and subtle flavour to this attractive dish.*

INGREDIENTS

*Serves 6*

15 g/½ oz/1 tbsp butter

225 g/8 oz cooked spinach, drained and chopped

150 ml/¼ pint/⅔ cup single cream

4 large eggs, separated

15 g/½ oz Parmesan cheese, grated

pinch of nutmeg

salt and freshly ground black pepper

*For the filling*

225 g/8 oz celeriac

lemon juice

75 g/3 oz St Agur cheese

115 g/4 oz fromage frais

1 Preheat the oven to 200°C/400°F/Gas 6. Line a 33 x 23 cm/13 x 9 in Swiss roll tin with non-stick baking parchment.

2 Melt the butter in a saucepan and add the spinach. Cook until all the liquid has evaporated. Remove the pan from the heat. Stir in the cream, egg yolks, Parmesan and nutmeg. Season.

3 Whisk the egg whites until stiff, fold them gently into the spinach mixture and then spoon into the prepared tin. Spread the mixture evenly and use a palette knife to smooth the surface.

4 Bake for 10–15 minutes, until the roulade is firm to the touch. Turn out on to a sheet of greaseproof paper and peel away the lining paper. Roll up the roulade with the greaseproof paper inside and leave to cool slightly.

5 To make the filling, peel the celeriac and grate it into a bowl. Sprinkle with lemon juice to taste. Blend the St Agur cheese and fromage frais together and mix with the celeriac and a little black pepper.

6 Unroll the roulade, spread with the filling and roll up again, this time without the paper. Serve at once or wrap loosely and chill.

# Dry Goods

*Building up a store cupboard of everyday items such as flours, grains and pasta will ensure that you can produce a speedy meal at short notice.*

### Barley
With its distinctive flavour and slightly chewy texture, barley is used in soups or as an alternative to rice in risottos.

### Buckwheat
Nutty in texture, this tasty alternative to rice is actually a grass.

### Bulgur wheat
This wholewheat grain is steam-dried and cracked before sale, so it only needs a brief soaking before use. Keep it cool and dry in the cupboard, and it will last for a few months.

### Couscous
Also made from wheat, this grain is a staple in North Africa and is prepared in exactly the same way as bulgur.

### Dried fruit
Rich in dietary fibre, vitamins and minerals, dried fruits are delicious in a wide selection of dishes including muesli and pies. Because of their intense sweetness, they can be used as a healthy alternative to sugar in cooking.

### Flours
As well as the usual white refined flour, try experimenting with other types including wholemeal, buckwheat, soya, rice or rye for a more interesting, nutty flavour in your baking. Cornflour is often used as a thickening agent for sauces.

### Millet
High in protein, millet is used extensively in Southeast Asia and is cooked in the same way as rice.

### Nuts and seeds
Nuts and seeds such as almond, cashew, brazil, sunflower, pumpkin and linseed are a valuable source of protein, calcium and Omega 3 fatty acids. Bought in bulk for economy, they will keep in the freezer for several months.

### Oats
Available as rolled (porridge), jumbo or oatmeal, this grain is an excellent source of complex carbohydrates, vitamins and minerals, including iron.

### Pasta
While fresh pasta is generally preferred both for flavour and for speed of cooking, the dried product is a very valuable store-cupboard ingredient. Italian pasta and Oriental noodles are both useful.

### Quinoa
This good source of protein, is a soft grain from South America.

### Rice
There are many different types of rice. Basmati is thought to have a superior flavour, fragrance and texture, and a mixture of basmati and wild rice (not a true rice, but the seeds of an aquatic grass) works well.

### Sugars
Used sparingly, you can give flavour to sweet dishes by adding dried sugars such as molasses, demerara, raw cane and icing sugar, or liquid varieties such as blackstrap molasses, honey and natural maple syrup.

### Wheat, barley and rye flakes
These can be used in savoury or sweet crumbles and biscuits to provide taste and texture.

# Goat's Cheese Soufflé

*Make sure everyone is seated before
the soufflé comes out of the oven
because it will begin to deflate
almost immediately. The recipe
works equally well with strong blue
cheeses such as Roquefort.*

### INGREDIENTS

*Serves 4–6*

40 g/1½ oz/3 tbsp butter

25 g/1 oz/¼ cup plain flour

175 ml/6 fl oz/¾ cup milk

1 bay leaf

freshly grated nutmeg

grated Parmesan cheese, for sprinkling

40 g/1½ oz herb and garlic soft cheese

150 g/5 oz firm goat's cheese, diced

6 egg whites, at room temperature

1.5 ml/¼ tsp cream of tartar

salt and freshly ground black pepper

1 Melt 25 g/1 oz/2 tbsp butter in
a heavy saucepan over medium
heat. Add the flour and cook until
golden, stirring occasionally.

2 Pour in half the milk, stirring
vigorously until smooth. Stir
in the remaining milk and add the
bay leaf. Season with a pinch of salt
and plenty of pepper and nutmeg.
Reduce the heat to medium low,
cover and simmer gently for about
5 minutes, stirring occasionally.

3 Preheat the oven to
190°C/375°F/Gas 5.
Generously butter a 1.5 litre/
2½ pint/6¼ cup soufflé dish and
sprinkle with Parmesan cheese.

4 Remove the sauce from the
heat and discard the bay leaf.
Stir in both cheeses.

5 In a clean greasefree bowl,
using an electric mixer or
balloon whisk, beat the egg whites
slowly until they become frothy.
Add the cream of tartar, increase
the speed and continue beating
until they form soft peaks, then
stiffer peaks that just flop over a
little at the top.

6 Stir a spoonful of beaten egg
whites into the cheese sauce to
lighten it, then pour the cheese
sauce over the remaining whites.
Using a large metal spoon, gently
fold the sauce into the whites until
the mixtures are just combined.

7 Pour the soufflé mixture into
the prepared dish and bake for
25–30 minutes, until puffed and
golden brown. Serve at once.

# Bottled and Canned Goods

*The store cupboard should be the backbone of your vegetarian kitchen. Stock it sensibly, and you'll always have the wherewithal to make a tasty, satisfying meal.*

### Canned pulses

Chick-peas, cannellini beans, green lentils, haricot beans and red kidney beans survive the canning process well. Wash in cold running water and drain well before use.

### Canned vegetables

Although fresh vegetables are best for most cooking, some canned products are very useful. Artichoke hearts have a mild sweet flavour and are great for adding to stir-fries, salads, risottos or pizzas. Pimientos are canned whole red peppers, seeded and peeled. Canned tomatoes are an essential ingredient to have in the pantry. Additional useful items to include are sweetcorn and water chestnuts.

### Mustard

Wholegrain or Dijon mustards are widely used both in cooking and in salad dressings.

### Oils

Groundnut or sunflower oils are bland and will not mask or overpower delicate flavours. They are ideal for deep frying. Fiery chilli oil will liven up vegetable stir-fries, while tasty sesame oil will give them a rich nutty flavour. A good olive oil will suit most purposes, except deep frying, and extra-virgin olive oil, being more expensive, is best kept for salads.

### Olives

Green or black olives now come in a variety of marinades. Olive paste is useful for pasta sauces.

### Passata

This thick sauce is made from sieved tomatoes. It is mainly used in Italian cookery.

### Pesto

This classic Italian sauce combines fresh basil, pine nuts, Parmesan, garlic and olive oil and is useful for pasta or grilled or roasted vegetables.

### Soy sauce/Shoyu

Soy sauce is a thin, salty black liquid made from fermented soya beans. Shoyu, or naturally brewed soy sauce, is fermented for far longer and so has less additives than soy sauce.

### Stocks and flavourings

There are three kinds of vegetable stocks. Granules are ideal for light soups and risottos, stock cubes have a stronger flavour suited to hearty soups, while vegetable extracts have a robust taste which is delicious in casseroles.

### Sun-dried tomatoes

These sweet tomatoes, baked and dried in the sun, are sold in bags or in jars, steeped in olive oil.

### Tahini paste

Made from ground sesame seeds, this paste is used in Middle Eastern cookery.

### Tomato purée

This concentrated tomato paste is sold in cans, jars or tubes. A version made from sun-dried tomatoes is now available.

### Vinegars

White or red wine and sherry vinegars are ideal for salad dressings. Balsamic has a sweet/sour flavour which can be used in salad dressings or with roasted vegetables and cooked grains.

# Leek Soufflé

*Soufflés are a great way to impress guests at a dinner party. This one is simple to make but it looks very sophisticated.*

INGREDIENTS

*Serves 2–3*

15 g/½ oz/1 tbsp butter

15 ml/1 tbsp sunflower oil

40 g/1½ oz/3 tbsp butter

2 leeks, thinly sliced

about 300 ml/½ pint/1¼ cups milk

25 g/1 oz/¼ cup plain flour

4 eggs, separated

75 g/3 oz Gruyère or Emmenthal cheese, grated

salt and freshly ground black pepper

1 Preheat the oven to 180°C/350°F/Gas 4. Butter a large soufflé dish. Heat the sunflower oil and 15 g/½ oz/1 tbsp of the butter in a small saucepan or flameproof casserole and fry the leeks over gentle heat for 4–5 minutes, until soft but not brown.

2 Stir in the milk and bring to the boil. Cover and simmer for 4–5 minutes, until the leeks are tender. Strain the liquid through a sieve into a measuring jug.

3 Melt the remaining butter, stir in the flour and cook for 1 minute. Remove from the heat.

4 Make up the reserved liquid with milk to 300 ml/½ pint/1¼ cups. Gradually stir in the milk to make a smooth sauce. Return to the heat and bring to the boil, stirring. When thickened, remove from the heat. Cool slightly and beat in the egg yolks, cheese and leeks.

5 Whisk the egg whites until stiff and, using a large metal spoon, fold into the leek and egg mixture. Pour into the prepared soufflé dish and bake for about 30 minutes, until puffed and golden brown. Serve immediately.

# SOUPS

# Grilled Vegetable Terrine

*Impress your guests with a colourful layered terrine using a mixture of Mediterranean vegetables.*

INGREDIENTS

*Serves 6*

2 large red peppers, quartered, cored
    and seeded
2 large yellow peppers, quartered, cored
    and seeded
1 large aubergine, sliced lengthways
2 large courgettes, sliced lengthways
90 ml/6 tbsp olive oil
1 large red onion, thinly sliced
75 g/3 oz/½ cup raisins
15 ml/1 tbsp tomato purée
15 ml/1 tbsp red wine vinegar
400 ml/14 fl oz/1⅔ cups tomato juice
15 g/½ oz/2 tbsp vegetarian gelatine
fresh basil leaves, to garnish

*For the dressing*
90 ml/6 tbsp olive oil
30 ml/2 tbsp red wine vinegar
salt and freshly ground black pepper

1 Place the peppers skin side up under a hot grill and cook until blackened. Put in a bowl. Cover.

2 Arrange the aubergine and courgette slices on separate baking sheets. Brush them with oil and cook under the grill.

3 Heat the remaining olive oil in a frying pan. Add the onion, raisins, tomato purée and red wine vinegar. Cook until soft.

4 Line a 1.75 litre/3 pint/7½ cup terrine with clear film.

5 Pour half the tomato juice into a saucepan. Sprinkle with the gelatine. Dissolve over a low heat.

6 Layer the red peppers in the terrine, and cover with some of the tomato juice and gelatine. Add the aubergine, courgettes, yellow peppers and onion mixture.

7 Pour tomato juice over each layer of vegetables and finish with another layer of red peppers.

8 Add the remaining tomato juice to any left in the pan and pour into the terrine. Give the terrine a sharp tap, to disperse the juice. Cover and chill in the refrigerator until set.

9 To make the dressing, whisk together the oil and vinegar. Season with salt and pepper.

10 Turn out the terrine and remove the clear film. Serve in thick slices, drizzled with dressing. Garnish with basil leaves.

# Wild Mushroom Soup

*Wild mushrooms are expensive, but dried porcini have an intense flavour, so only a small quantity is needed.*

INGREDIENTS

*Serves 4*

25 g/1 oz/2 cups dried porcini mushrooms

30 ml/2 tbsp olive oil

15 g/½ oz/1 tbsp butter

2 leeks, thinly sliced

2 shallots, roughly chopped

1 garlic clove, roughly chopped

225 g/8 oz fresh wild mushrooms

about 1.2 litres/2 pints/5 cups vegetable stock

2.5 ml/½ tsp dried thyme

150 ml/¼ pint/⅔ cup double cream

salt and freshly ground black pepper

sprigs of fresh thyme, to garnish

1 Put the dried porcini in a bowl, add 250 ml/8 fl oz/1 cup warm water and leave to soak for 20–30 minutes. Lift out of the liquid and squeeze over the bowl to remove as much of the soaking liquid as possible. Strain all the liquid and reserve to use later. Finely chop the porcini.

2 Heat the oil and butter in a large saucepan until foaming. Add the sliced leeks, chopped shallots and garlic and cook gently for about 5 minutes, stirring frequently, until softened but not coloured.

3 Chop or slice the fresh mushrooms and add to the pan. Stir over a medium heat for a few minutes until they begin to soften. Pour in the stock and bring to the boil. Add the porcini, soaking liquid, dried thyme and salt and pepper. Lower the heat, half cover the pan and simmer gently for 30 minutes, stirring occasionally.

4 Pour about three-quarters of the soup into a blender or food processor and process until smooth. Return the processed soup to the soup remaining in the pan, stir in the cream and heat through. Check the consistency and add more stock if necessary. Season with salt and pepper. Serve hot, garnished with thyme sprigs.

---

### COOK'S TIP

Porcini are ceps. Italian cooks would make this soup with a combination of fresh and dried ceps, but if fresh ceps are difficult to obtain, you can use other wild mushrooms such as chanterelles.

# Greek Filo Twists

*Spinach and feta cheese make up the secret filling hidden inside these pretty filo parcels.*

### INGREDIENTS

*Serves 4*

15 ml/1 tbsp olive oil

1 small onion, finely chopped

275 g/10 oz fresh spinach, stalks removed

50 g/2 oz/4 tbsp butter, melted

4 sheets filo pastry (about 45 x 25 cm/
    18 x 10 in)

1 egg

pinch of grated nutmeg

75 g/3 oz/¼ cup crumbled feta cheese

15 ml/1 tbsp freshly grated Parmesan
    cheese

salt and freshly ground black pepper

1 Preheat the oven to 190°C/375°F/Gas 5. Heat the oil in a pan, add the onion and fry gently for 5–6 minutes, until softened.

2 Add the spinach leaves and cook, stirring, until the spinach has wilted and some of the liquid has evaporated. Leave to cool.

3 Brush four 10 cm/4 in diameter loose-based tartlet tins with a little melted butter. Take two sheets of the filo pastry and cut each into eight 12 cm/4½ in squares. Keep the remaining sheets covered.

4 Brush four squares at a time with melted butter. Line the first tartlet tin with one square, gently easing it into the base and up the sides. Leave the edges overhanging.

5 Lay the remaining three buttered squares on top of the first, turning them so the corners form a star shape. Repeat for the remaining tartlet tins.

6 Beat the egg with the nutmeg and season with salt and pepper. Stir in the cheeses and spinach. Divide the mixture between the tins and smooth the tops. Fold the overhanging pastry back over the filling.

7 Cut one of the remaining sheets of pastry into eight 10 cm/4 in rounds. Brush with butter and place two on top of each tartlet. Press around the edges to seal. Brush the remaining sheet of pastry with butter and cut into strips. Twist each strip and lay on top of the tartlets. Leave to stand for 5 minutes, then bake for 30–35 minutes. Serve hot or cold.

# Tomato and Fresh Basil Soup

*A pungent soup for late summer when fresh tomatoes are at their most flavoursome.*

INGREDIENTS

*Serves 4–6*

15 ml/1 tbsp olive oil

25 g/1 oz/2 tbsp butter

1 medium onion, finely chopped

900 g/2 1b ripe Italian plum tomatoes, roughly chopped

1 garlic clove, roughly chopped

about 750 ml/1¼ pints/3 cups vegetable stock

120 ml/4 fl oz/½ cup dry white wine

30 ml/2 tbsp sun-dried tomato paste

30 ml/2 tbsp shredded fresh basil

150 ml/¼ pint/⅔ cup double cream

salt and freshly ground black pepper

whole basil leaves, to garnish

1 Heat the oil and butter in a large saucepan until foaming. Add the onion and cook gently for about 5 minutes, stirring, until the onion is softened but not brown.

2 Stir in the chopped tomatoes and garlic, then add the stock, white wine and sun-dried tomato paste, with salt and pepper to taste. Bring to the boil, then lower the heat, half cover the pan and simmer gently for 20 minutes, stirring occasionally to stop the tomatoes sticking to the base of the pan.

3 Process the soup with the shredded basil in a blender or food processor, then press through a sieve into a clean pan.

4 Add the double cream and heat through, stirring. Do not allow the soup to approach boiling point. Check the consistency and add more stock if necessary and then season with salt and pepper. Pour into heated bowls and garnish with basil. Serve at once.

# Buckwheat Blinis with Mushroom Caviar

*These little Russian pancakes are traditionally served with fish roe caviar and soured cream. The term caviar is also given to fine vegetable mixtures called ikry. This wild mushroom ikry has a rich and silky texture.*

## INGREDIENTS

*Serves 4*

115 g/4 oz/1 cup strong white bread flour

50 g/2 oz/⅓ cup buckwheat flour

2.5 ml/½ tsp salt

300 ml/½ pint/1¼ cups milk

5 ml/1 tsp dried yeast

2 eggs, separated

200 ml/7 fl oz/⅞ cup soured cream or crème fraîche, to serve

*For the caviar*

350 g/12 oz assorted wild mushrooms, such as field mushrooms, orange birch bolete, bay boletus, oyster and St George's mushrooms

5 ml/1 tsp celery salt

30 ml/2 tbsp walnut oil

15 ml/1 tbsp lemon juice

45 ml/3 tbsp chopped fresh parsley

freshly ground black pepper

1 To make the caviar, trim and chop the mushrooms and place them in a glass bowl. Toss with the celery salt and cover with a weighted plate.

2 Leave the mushrooms for 2 hours, until the juices have run out into the bottom of the bowl. Rinse them thoroughly to remove the salt.

3 Drain and press out as much liquid as you can with the back of a spoon. Return them to the bowl and toss with the walnut oil, lemon juice and parsley. Season with pepper and chill until ready to serve.

4 Sift the two flours together with the salt in a large mixing bowl. Warm the milk to approximately blood temperature. Add the yeast, stirring until dissolved, then pour into the flour. Add the egg yolks and stir to make a smooth batter. Cover with a damp cloth and leave in a warm place to rise, for about 30 minutes.

5 Whisk the egg whites in a clean bowl until stiff, then fold into the risen batter.

6 Heat an iron pan to moderate temperature. Moisten with oil, then drop spoonfuls of the batter on to the surface, turn them over and cook briefly on the other side. Spoon on the mushroom caviar and serve with the soured cream.

# Cream of Courgette Soup

*The beauty of this soup is its delicate colour, rich and creamy texture and subtle taste. If you prefer a more pronounced cheese flavour, use Gorgonzola instead of dolcelatte.*

### INGREDIENTS

*Serves 4–6*

30 ml/2 tbsp olive oil

15 g/½ oz/1 tbsp butter

1 medium onion, roughly chopped

900 g/2 lb courgettes, trimmed and sliced

5 ml/1 tsp dried oregano

about 600 ml/1 pint/2½ cups
    vegetable stock

115 g/4 oz dolcelatte cheese, rind
    removed, diced

300 ml/½ pint/1¼ cups single cream

salt and freshly ground black pepper

fresh oregano, extra dolcelatte and cream,
    to garnish

2 Add the courgettes and oregano with salt and pepper to taste. Cook over a medium heat for 10 minutes, stirring frequently. Pour in the stock and bring to the boil, stirring.

3 Lower the heat, half cover the pan and simmer gently, stirring occasionally, for about 30 minutes. Stir in the diced dolcelatte until melted.

4 Process the soup in a blender or food processor until smooth, then press through a sieve into a clean pan.

5 Add two-thirds of the cream and stir over a low heat until hot, but not boiling. Add more stock or water if the soup is too thick. Season with salt and pepper. Pour into heated bowls. Swirl in the remaining cream. Serve, garnished with oregano, extra cheese, cream and pepper.

1 Heat the oil and butter in a large saucepan until foaming. Add the onion and cook gently for about 5 minutes, stirring frequently, until softened but not brown.

### COOK'S TIP

To save time, trim off and discard the ends of the courgettes, cut them into thirds, then chop in a food processor fitted with a metal blade.

# Fonduta with Steamed Vegetables

Fonduta is a creamy cheese sauce from Italy. Traditionally it is garnished with slices of white truffles and eaten with toasted bread rounds.

INGREDIENTS

*Serves 4*

assorted vegetables, such as fennel, broccoli, carrots, cauliflower and courgettes
115 g/4 oz/8 tbsp butter
12–16 rounds of Italian or French baguette

*For the fonduta*

300 g/11 oz/1⅔ cups fontina cheese
15 ml/1 tbsp flour
milk, as required
50 g/2 oz/4 tbsp butter
50 g/2 oz/½ cup freshly grated Parmesan cheese
pinch of grated nutmeg
2 egg yolks, at room temperature
a few slivers of white truffle (optional)
salt and freshly ground black pepper

1 About 6 hours before you want to serve the fonduta, cut the fontina into chunks and place in a bowl. Sprinkle with the flour. Pour in enough milk to barely cover the cheese and set aside in a cool place. The cheese should be at room temperature before being cooked.

2 Just before preparing the fonduta, steam the vegetables until tender. Cut into pieces. Place on a serving platter, dot with butter and keep warm.

3 Butter the bread and toast lightly in the oven or under the grill.

4 For the fonduta, melt the butter in a bowl set over a pan of simmering water, or in a double boiler. Strain the fontina and add it, with 45–60 ml/3–4 tbsp of its soaking milk. Cook, stirring, until the cheese melts. When it is hot, and has formed a homogeneous mass, add the Parmesan and stir until melted. Season with nutmeg, salt and pepper.

5 Remove from the heat and immediately beat in the egg yolks, which have previously been passed through a sieve. Spoon into warmed individual serving bowls, garnish with white truffle, if using, and serve with the vegetables and toasted bread.

# Garlic, Chick-pea and Spinach Soup

*This delicious, thick and creamy soup is richly flavoured and makes a great one-pot meal.*

*Serves 4*

30 ml/2 tbsp olive oil

4 garlic cloves, crushed

1 onion, roughly chopped

10 ml/2 tsp ground cumin

10 ml/2 tsp ground coriander

1.2 litres/2 pints/5 cups vegetable stock

350 g/12 oz potatoes, peeled and
  finely chopped

425 g/15 oz can chick-peas, drained

15 ml/1 tbsp cornflour

150 ml/¼ pint/⅔ cup double cream

30 ml/2 tbsp light tahini (sesame
  seed paste)

200 g/7 oz spinach, shredded

cayenne pepper

salt and freshly ground black pepper

1 Heat the oil in a large saucepan and cook the garlic and onion for 5 minutes, or until they are softened and golden brown.

2 Stir in the cumin and coriander and cook for a further minute.

3 Pour in the stock and add the chopped potatoes to the pan. Bring to the boil and simmer for 10 minutes. Add the chick-peas and simmer for a further 5 minutes, or until the potatoes and chick-peas are just tender.

4 Blend together the cornflour, cream, tahini and plenty of seasoning. Stir into the soup with the spinach. Bring to the boil, stirring, and simmer for a further 2 minutes. Season with cayenne pepper, salt and black pepper. Serve immediately, sprinkled with a little cayenne pepper.

# Broccoli Timbales

*This elegant but easy to make dish can be made with almost any puréed vegetable, such as carrot or celeriac. To avoid last-minute fuss, make the timbales a few hours ahead and cook while the first course is being eaten. Or serve them on their own as a starter with a little white wine butter sauce.*

### INGREDIENTS

*Serves 4*

15 g/½ oz/1 tbsp butter

350 g/12 oz broccoli florets

45 ml/3 tbsp crème fraiche or
    whipping cream

1 egg, plus one egg yolk

15 ml/1 tbsp chopped spring onion

pinch of freshly grated nutmeg

salt and freshly ground black pepper

white wine butter sauce, to serve
    (optional)

fresh chives, to garnish (optional)

1 Preheat the oven to 190°C/375°F/Gas 5. Lightly butter four 175 ml/6 fl oz/¾ cup ramekins. Line the bases with greaseproof paper and butter the paper.

2 Steam the broccoli in the top of a covered steamer over boiling water for 8–10 minutes, until very tender.

3 Put the broccoli in a food processor fitted with the metal blade and process with the cream, egg and egg yolk until smooth.

4 Add the spring onion and season with salt, pepper and nutmeg. Pulse to mix.

5 Spoon the purée into the ramekins and place in a roasting tin. Add boiling water to come halfway up the sides. Bake for 25 minutes, until just set. Invert on to warmed plates and peel off the paper. If serving as a starter, pour sauce around each timbale and garnish with chives.

# Classic French Onion Soup

*When French onion soup is made slowly and carefully, the onions almost caramelize to a deep mahogany colour. It has a superb flavour and is a perfect winter supper dish.*

*Serves 4*

4 large onions

30 ml/2 tbsp sunflower or olive oil, or 15ml/1 tbsp of each

25 g/1 oz/2 tbsp butter

900 ml/1½ pints/3¾ cups vegetable stock

4 slices French bread

40–50 g/1½–2 oz Gruyère or Cheddar cheese, grated

salt and freshly ground black pepper

1 Peel and quarter the onions and slice or chop them into 5 mm/¼ in pieces. Heat the oil and butter in a deep saucepan, preferably with a medium-size base so that the onions form a thick layer.

2 Fry the onions briskly for a few minutes, stirring constantly.

3 Reduce the heat and cook gently for 45–60 minutes. At first, the onions need to be stirred only occasionally but as they begin to colour, stir frequently. The colour of the onions gradually turns golden and then more rapidly to brown, so take care to stir constantly at this stage so that they do not burn on the base.

4 When the onions are a rich mahogany brown, add the vegetable stock and a little seasoning. Simmer, partially covered, for 30 minutes, then season with salt and pepper.

5 Preheat the grill and toast the French bread. Spoon the soup into four ovenproof serving dishes and place a piece of bread in each. Sprinkle with the cheese and grill for a few minutes until golden. Season with plenty of freshly ground black pepper.

# SPECIAL
# OCCASIONS

~

# White Bean Soup

*A thick purée of cooked dried beans is at the heart of this substantial country soup from Tuscany. It makes a warming lunch or supper dish.*

### INGREDIENTS

*Serves 6*

350 g/12 oz/1½ cups dried cannellini or
   other white beans
1 bay leaf
75 ml/5 tbsp olive oil
1 medium onion, finely chopped
1 carrot, finely chopped
1 stick celery, finely chopped
3 medium tomatoes, peeled and finely
   chopped
2 cloves garlic, finely chopped
5 ml/1 tsp fresh thyme leaves or 2.5 ml/
   ½ tsp dried thyme
750 ml/1¼ pints/3 cups boiling water
salt and freshly ground black pepper
olive oil, to serve

1 Pick over the beans carefully, discarding any stones or other particles. Rinse thoroughly in cold water to ensure that they are clean. Soak in a large bowl of cold water overnight. Drain the beans and place them in a large saucepan of water, bring to the boil and cook for 20 minutes. Drain. Return the beans to the pan, cover with cold water and bring to the boil again. Add the bay leaf and cook until the beans are tender for approximately 1–2 hours. Drain again. Remove the bay leaf.

2 Purée about three-quarters of the beans in a food processor, or pass through a food mill, adding a little water if necessary, to create a smooth paste.

3 Heat the oil in a large saucepan. Stir in the onion and cook until it softens. Add the carrot and celery, and cook for 5 minutes more.

4 Stir in the tomatoes, garlic and thyme. Cook for 6–8 minutes more, stirring often.

5 Pour in the boiling water. Stir in the beans and the bean purée. Season with salt and pepper. Simmer for 10–15 minutes. Serve in individual soup bowls, sprinkled with a little olive oil.

### COOK'S TIP

Other types of canned cooked beans, such as cannellini or borlotti, may be substituted in this recipe. Simply drain the beans and omit Step 1.

# Roquefort and Walnut Pasta Salad

*This is a simple earthy salad, relying totally on the quality of the ingredients. There is no real substitute for Roquefort – a blue-veined ewe's-milk cheese which comes from south-western France.*

INGREDIENTS

*Serves 4*

225g/8oz pasta shapes

mixed salad leaves, such as rocket, curly
   endive, lamb's lettuce, baby spinach,
   radicchio, etc

30ml/2 tbsp walnut oil

60ml/4 tbsp sunflower oil

30ml/2 tbsp red wine vinegar or
   sherry vinegar

225g/8oz Roquefort cheese,
   roughly crumbled

115g/4oz/1 cup walnut halves

salt and ground black pepper

1 Cook the pasta in plenty of boiling salted water according to the instructions on the packet. Drain well and cool. Wash and dry the salad leaves and place them in a large bowl.

2 Whisk together the walnut oil, sunflower oil, vinegar and salt and pepper to taste.

4 Scatter over the walnuts. Toss just before serving.

3 Pile the pasta in the centre of the leaves, scatter over the crumbled Roquefort and pour over the dressing.

---

COOK'S TIP

Try toasting the walnuts under the grill for a couple of minutes to release the flavour.

---

# Asparagus Soup

*Home-made asparagus soup has a delicate flavour, quite unlike that from a can. This soup is best made with young asparagus, which are tender and blend well. Serve it with wafer-thin slices of bread.*

*Serves 4*

450 g/1 lb young asparagus

40 g/1½ oz/3 tbsp butter

6 shallots, sliced

15 g/½ oz/1 tbsp plain flour

600 ml/1 pint/2½ cups vegetable stock or
    water

15 ml/1 tbsp lemon juice

250 ml/8 fl oz/1 cup milk

120 ml/4 fl oz/½ cup single cream

10 ml/2 tsp chopped fresh chervil

salt and freshly ground black pepper

1 Cut 4 cm/1½ in off the tops of half the asparagus and set aside for a garnish. Slice the remaining asparagus.

2 Melt 25 g/1 oz/2 tbsp of the butter in a large saucepan and fry the sliced shallots for 2–3 minutes until soft.

3 Add the asparagus and fry over a low heat for about 1 minute.

4 Stir in the flour and cook for 1 minute. Stir in the stock or water and lemon juice and season with salt and pepper. Bring to the boil, half cover the pan, then simmer for 15–20 minutes, until the asparagus is very tender.

5 Cool slightly and then process the soup in a food processor or blender until smooth. Press the puréed asparagus through a sieve into a clean saucepan. Add the milk by pouring and stirring it through the sieve with the asparagus so as to extract the maximum amount of asparagus purée.

6 Melt the remaining butter and fry the reserved asparagus tips gently for 3–4 minutes to soften.

7 Heat the soup gently for 3–4 minutes. Stir in the cream and the asparagus tips. Continue to heat gently and serve sprinkled with chopped fresh chervil.

# Curly Spaghetti with Walnut and Cream

*A classic Italian dish with a strong, nutty flavour, this should be served with a delicately flavoured salad.*

INGREDIENTS

*Serves 4*

350g/12oz curly spaghetti (fusilli
   col buco)
50g/2oz/½ cup walnut pieces
25g/1oz/2 tbsp butter
300ml/½ pint/1¼ cups milk
50g/2oz/1 cup fresh breadcrumbs
25g/1oz/2 tbsp freshly grated
   Parmesan cheese
pinch of freshly grated nutmeg
salt and ground black pepper
fresh rosemary sprigs, to garnish

1 Cook the pasta in plenty of boiling salted water according to the instructions on the packet. Meanwhile, preheat the grill.

2 Spread the walnuts evenly over the grill pan. Grill for about 5 minutes, turning occasionally until evenly toasted.

3 Remove the walnuts from the heat, place in a clean dish towel and rub away the skins. Roughly chop the nuts.

4 Heat the butter and milk in a saucepan until the butter is completely melted.

5 Stir in the breadcrumbs and nuts and heat gently for 2 minutes, stirring constantly until thickened.

6 Add the Parmesan cheese, nutmeg and seasoning to taste.

7 Drain the pasta thoroughly through a colander and toss in the sauce. Serve immediately, garnished with fresh sprigs of rosemary.

# Fresh Tomato, Lentil and Onion Soup

*This delicious wholesome soup is ideal served with thick slices of wholemeal or granary bread.*

Serves 4–6

10 ml/2 tsp sunflower oil

1 large onion, chopped

2 sticks celery, chopped

175 g/6 oz/¾ cup split red lentils

2 large tomatoes, skinned and roughly chopped

900 ml/1½ pints/3¾ cups vegetable stock

10 ml/2 tsp dried herbes de Provence

salt and freshly ground black pepper

chopped parsley, to garnish

1 Heat the oil in a large saucepan. Add the onion and celery and cook for 5 minutes, stirring occasionally. Add the lentils and cook for 1 minute.

2 Stir in the tomatoes, stock, dried herbs, salt and pepper. Cover, bring to the boil and simmer for about 20 minutes, stirring occasionally.

3 When the lentils are cooked and tender, set the soup aside to cool slightly.

4 Purée in a blender or food processor until smooth. Season with salt and pepper, return to the saucepan and reheat gently until piping hot. Ladle into soup bowls to serve and garnish each with chopped parsley.

# Pappardelle, with Beans and Mushrooms

*A mixture of wild and cultivated mushrooms help to give this dish a rich and nutty flavour.*

*Serves 4*

30ml/2 tbsp olive oil

50g/2oz/4 tbsp butter

2 shallots, chopped

2–3 garlic cloves, crushed

675g/1½lb mixed mushrooms,
   thickly sliced

4 sun-dried tomatoes in oil, drained
   and chopped

90ml/6 tbsp dry white wine

400g/14oz can borlotti beans, drained

45ml/3 tbsp grated Parmesan cheese

chopped fresh parsley, to garnish

salt and ground black pepper

cooked pappardelle, to serve

1 Heat the oil and butter in a frying pan and fry the shallots until they are soft.

2 Add the garlic and mushrooms and fry for 3–4 minutes. Stir in the sun-dried tomatoes, wine and add seasoning to taste.

3 Stir in the borlotti beans and cook for 5–6 minutes, until most of the liquid has evaporated from the pan and the beans are warmed through.

4 Stir in the grated Parmesan cheese. Sprinkle with parsley and serve immediately with freshly cooked pappardelle.

# Split Pea and Courgette Soup

*Rich and satisfying, this tasty and nutritious soup will warm a chilly winter's day.*

*Serves 4*

175 g/6 oz/1⅞ cups yellow split peas
1 medium onion, finely chopped
5 ml/1 tsp sunflower oil
2 medium courgettes, finely diced
900 ml/1½ pints/3¾ cups vegetable stock
2.5 ml/½ tsp ground turmeric
salt and freshly ground black pepper
crusty bread, to serve

3 Add the remaining courgettes to the pan. Cook for 2–3 minutes. Add the stock and turmeric and bring to the boil. Reduce the heat, cover and simmer for 30–40 minutes. Season.

4 When the soup is almost ready, bring a large saucepan of water to the boil, add the reserved diced courgettes and cook for 1 minute. Drain and add to the soup. Serve hot with warm crusty bread.

1 Place the split peas in a bowl, cover with cold water and leave to soak for several hours or overnight. Drain, rinse in cold water and drain again.

2 Cook the onion in the oil in a covered pan, shaking occasionally, until soft. Reserve a handful of diced courgettes to use later.

## COOK'S TIP

For a quicker alternative, use red split lentils for this soup – they need no presoaking and cook very quickly. Adjust the amount of stock, if necessary.

# Tagliatelle with Gorgonzola Sauce

*Gorgonzola is a creamy Italian blue cheese. As an alternative you could use Danish Blue or Pipo Creme.*

INGREDIENTS

*Serves 4*

25g/1oz/2 tbsp butter, plus extra for
    tossing the pasta
225g/8oz Gorgonzola cheese
150ml/¼ pint/⅔ cup double or
    whipping cream
30ml/2 tbsp dry vermouth
5ml/1 tsp cornflour
15ml/1 tbsp chopped fresh sage
450g/1lb tagliatelle
salt and ground black pepper

1 Melt 25g/1oz/2 tbsp butter in a heavy saucepan (it needs to be thick-based to prevent the cheese from burning). Stir in 175g/6oz crumbled Gorgonzola cheese and stir over a gentle heat for about 2–3 minutes until melted.

2 Whisk in the cream, vermouth and cornflour. Add the sage; season. Cook, whisking, until the sauce boils and thickens. Set aside.

3 Boil the pasta in plenty of salted water according to the instructions on the packet. Drain well and toss with a little butter.

4 Reheat the sauce gently, whisking well. Divide the pasta among four serving bowls, top with the sauce and sprinkle over the remaining crumbled cheese. Serve immediately.

# Carrot and Coriander Soup

Nearly all root vegetables make excellent soups as they purée well and have an earthy flavour, which complements the sharper flavours of herbs and spices. Carrots are particularly versatile, and this simple soup is elegant in both flavour and appearance.

INGREDIENTS

Serves 4–6

450 g/1 lb carrots, preferably young and
    tender
15 ml/1 tbsp sunflower oil
40 g/1½ oz/3 tbsp butter
1 onion, chopped
1 stick celery, plus 2–3 pale leafy
    celery tops
2 small potatoes, peeled
1 litre/1¾ pints/4 cups vegetable stock
10-15 ml/2-3 tsp ground coriander
15 ml/1 tbsp chopped fresh coriander
200 ml/7 fl oz/⅞ cup milk
salt and freshly ground black pepper

1 Trim and peel the carrots and cut into chunks. Heat the oil and 25 g/1 oz/2 tbsp butter in a large flameproof casserole or heavy-based saucepan and fry the onion over a gentle heat for 3–4 minutes, until slightly softened.

2 Slice the celery and chop the potatoes. Add them to the onion in the pan, cook for a few minutes and then add the carrots. Fry over a gentle heat for 3–4 minutes, stirring, and then cover.

3 Reduce the heat even further and sweat for about 10 minutes. Shake the pan or stir occasionally so the vegetables do not stick to the base.

4 Add the stock and bring to the boil. Half cover the pan and simmer for a further 8–10 minutes, until the carrots and potatoes are tender.

5 Remove 6–8 tiny celery leaves for garnish and finely chop the remaining celery tops (about 15 ml/1 tbsp once chopped). Melt the remaining butter in a small saucepan and fry the ground coriander for about 1 minute, stirring constantly.

6 Reduce the heat and add the chopped celery tops and fresh coriander and fry for about 1 minute. Set aside.

7 Process the soup in a food processor or blender and pour into a clean saucepan. Stir in the milk and coriander mixture. Season, heat gently, taste and adjust seasoning. Serve garnished with the reserved celery leaves.

COOK'S TIP

For a more piquant flavour, add a little lemon juice just before serving.

*Soups*

21

# Baked Leeks with Cheese and Yogurt

*Like all vegetables, the fresher leeks are, the better their flavour, and the freshest leeks available should be used for this dish. Small, young leeks are around at the beginning of the season and are perfect to use here.*

INGREDIENTS

*Serves 4*

25 g/1 oz/2 tbsp butter

8 small leeks, about 675 g/1½ lb

2 small eggs or 1 large one, beaten

150 g/5 oz fresh goat's cheese

85 ml/3 fl oz/⅓ cup natural yogurt

50 g/2 oz Parmesan cheese, grated

25 g/1 oz/½ cup fresh white or brown
   breadcrumbs

salt and freshly ground black pepper

1 Preheat the oven to 180°C/350°F/Gas 4. Butter a shallow ovenproof dish. Trim the leeks, cut a slit from top to bottom and rinse well under cold water.

2 Place the leeks in a saucepan of water, bring to the boil and simmer gently for 6–8 minutes, until just tender. Remove and drain well using a slotted spoon. Arrange in the prepared dish.

3 Beat the eggs with the goat's cheese, yogurt and half the Parmesan cheese. Season well with salt and pepper.

4 Pour the cheese and yogurt mixture over the leeks. Mix the breadcrumbs and remaining Parmesan cheese together and sprinkle over the sauce. Bake for 35–40 minutes, until the top is crisp and golden brown.

# Fresh Pea Soup

This soup is known in France as Potage Saint-Germain, a name which comes from a suburb of Paris where peas used to be cultivated in market gardens. If fresh peas are not available, use frozen peas, but thaw and rinse them before use.

INGREDIENTS

Serves 2–3

25 g/1 oz/2 tbsp butter

2 or 3 shallots, finely chopped

400 g/14 oz/3 cups shelled fresh peas
   (from about 1.3 kg/3 lb garden peas) or
   thawed frozen peas

45-60 ml/3–4 tbsp whipping cream
   (optional)

salt and freshly ground black pepper

croûtons, to garnish

1 Melt the butter in a heavy saucepan or flameproof casserole. Add the shallots and cook for about 3 minutes, stirring occasionally.

2 Add 500 ml/16 fl oz/2 cups water and the peas, and season with salt and pepper.

3 Cover and simmer for 12 minutes for young or frozen peas and up to 18 minutes for large or older peas, stirring occasionally.

4 When the peas are tender, ladle them into a food processor or blender with a little of the cooking liquid and process until smooth.

5 Strain the soup into the saucepan or casserole, stir in the cream, if using, and heat through without boiling. Season with salt and pepper and serve hot garnished with croûtons.

# Spicy Jacket Potatoes

*Simple baked potatoes take on an exciting new character with the addition of a few herbs and spices.*

INGREDIENTS

*Serves 2–4*

2 large baking potatoes

5 ml/1 tsp sunflower oil

1 small onion, finely chopped

2.5 cm/1 in piece fresh root ginger, grated

5 ml/1 tsp ground cumin

5 ml/1 tsp ground coriander

2.5 ml/½ tsp ground turmeric

garlic salt

natural yogurt and sprigs of fresh
    coriander, to serve

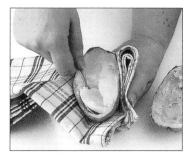

1 Preheat the oven to 190°C/375°F/Gas 5. Prick the potatoes with a fork. Bake for 1 hour, or until soft.

2 Cut the potatoes in half and scoop out the flesh. Heat the oil in a non-stick frying pan and fry the onion for a few minutes to soften. Stir in the ginger, cumin, coriander and turmeric.

3 Stir over a low heat for about 2 minutes, then add the potato flesh and garlic salt, to taste.

4 Cook the potato mixture for a further 2 minutes, stirring occasionally. Spoon the mixture back into the potato shells and top each with a spoonful of natural yogurt and a sprig or two of fresh coriander. Serve hot.

# Pea, Leek and Broccoli Soup

*A delicious and nutritious soup, ideal for warming those chilly winter evenings.*

INGREDIENTS

*Serves 4–6*

1 onion, chopped

225 g/8 oz/2 cups leeks (trimmed weight), sliced

225 g/8 oz unpeeled potatoes, diced

900 ml/1½ pints/3¾ cups vegetable stock

1 bay leaf

225 g/8 oz broccoli florets

175 g/6 oz/1½ cups frozen peas

30–45 ml/2–3 tbsp chopped fresh parsley

salt and freshly ground black pepper

parsley leaves, to garnish

1 Put the onion, leeks, potatoes, stock and bay leaf in a large saucepan and mix together. Cover, bring to the boil and simmer for 10 minutes, stirring.

2 Add the broccoli and peas, cover, return to the boil and simmer for a further 10 minutes, stirring occasionally.

3 Set aside to cool slightly and remove and discard the bay leaf. Purée in a blender or food processor until smooth.

4 Add the parsley, season with salt and pepper and process briefly. Return to the saucepan and reheat gently until piping hot. Ladle into soup bowls and garnish with parsley leaves.

# Spicy Chick-pea and Aubergine Stew

*This is a Lebanese dish that's full of the spicy flavours of the Middle East.*

## INGREDIENTS

*Serves 4*

3 large aubergines, cubed

200 g/7 oz/1 cup chick-peas,
    soaked overnight

60 ml/4 tbsp olive oil

3 garlic cloves, chopped

2 large onions, chopped

2.5 ml/½ tsp ground cumin

2.5 ml/½ tsp ground cinnamon

2.5 ml/½ tsp ground coriander

3 x 400 g/14 oz cans chopped tomatoes

salt and freshly ground black pepper

*For the garnish*

30 ml/2 tbsp olive oil

1 onion, sliced

1 garlic clove, sliced

sprigs of fresh coriander

1 Place the aubergines in a colander and sprinkle them with salt. Sit the colander in a bowl and leave for 30 minutes, to allow the bitter juices to escape. Rinse the aubergine with cold water and dry on kitchen paper.

2 Drain the chick-peas and put in a saucepan with enough water to cover. Bring to the boil and simmer for 1–1½ hours, or until tender. Drain.

3 Heat the oil in a large saucepan. Add the garlic and onion and cook until soft. Add the spices and cook, stirring, for a few seconds. Add the aubergine and stir. Cook for 5 minutes. Add the tomatoes and chick-peas and season with salt and pepper. Cover and simmer for 20 minutes.

4 To make the garnish, heat the oil in a frying pan and, when very hot, add the sliced onion and garlic. Fry until golden and crisp. Serve the stew with rice, topped with the onion and garlic and garnished with coriander.

# Gazpacho

This cold soup is popular all over Spain, where there are hundreds of variations. It uses tomatoes, tomato juice, green pepper and garlic, and is served with a selection of garnishes.

*Serves 4*

1.5 kg/3–3½ lb ripe tomatoes
1 green pepper, seeded and
    roughly chopped
2 garlic cloves, crushed
2 slices white bread, crusts removed
60 ml/4 tbsp olive oil
60 ml/4 tbsp tarragon wine vinegar
150 ml/¼ pint/⅔ cup tomato juice
good pinch of sugar
salt and freshly ground black pepper
ice cubes, to serve

*For the garnishes*

30 ml/2 tbsp sunflower oil
2–3 slices white bread, diced
1 small cucumber, peeled and finely diced
1 small onion, finely chopped
1 red pepper, seeded and finely diced
1 green pepper, seeded and finely diced
2 hard-boiled eggs, chopped

1 Skin and quarter the tomatoes, then remove the cores.

2 Place the pepper in a food processor and process for a few seconds. Add the tomatoes, garlic, bread, olive oil and vinegar and process again. Add the tomato juice, sugar, salt and pepper and process.

3 The mixture should be thick but not too stodgy. Continue processing until it is the right consistency. Press the liquid through a sieve into a bowl and chill for at least 2 hours but no more than 12 hours, otherwise the texture will deteriorate.

4 To prepare the bread cubes to use as a garnish, heat the oil in a frying pan and fry them over a moderate heat for 4–5 minutes, until golden brown. Drain well on kitchen paper.

5 Place each garnish in a separate small dish, or alternatively arrange them in rows on a large plate.

6 Just before serving, stir a few ice cubes into the soup and then spoon into serving bowls. Serve with the garnishes.

# Provençal Stuffed Peppers

*Stuffed peppers are easy to make for
a light and healthy supper.*

*Serves 4*

15 ml/1 tbsp olive oil

1 red onion, sliced

1 courgette, diced

115 g/4 oz mushrooms, sliced

1 garlic clove, crushed

400 g/14 oz can chopped tomatoes

15 ml/1 tbsp tomato purée

40 g/1½ oz/scant ⅓ cup pine nuts

30 ml/2 tbsp chopped fresh basil

4 large yellow peppers

50 g/2 oz/½ cup red Leicester cheese,
    finely grated

salt and freshly ground black pepper

fresh basil leaves, to garnish

2 Stir in the tomatoes and
tomato purée, then bring to
the boil and simmer, uncovered,
for 10–15 minutes, stirring occasionally, until thickened slightly.
Remove from the heat and stir in
the pine nuts, basil and seasoning.

3 Cut the peppers in half lengthways and seed them. Blanch in
a pan of boiling water for about
3 minutes. Drain.

4 Place the peppers in a shallow
ovenproof dish and fill with
the vegetable mixture.

5 Cover the dish with foil and
bake for 20 minutes. Uncover,
sprinkle each pepper with grated
cheese and bake for a further 5–10
minutes, until the cheese is melted
and bubbling. Garnish with basil
leaves and serve.

1 Preheat the oven to
180°C/350°F/Gas 4. Heat the
oil in a saucepan, add the onion,
courgette, mushrooms and garlic
and cook gently for 3 minutes,
stirring occasionally.

### VARIATION

Use the vegetable filling to stuff
other vegetables, such as
courgettes or aubergines, in
place of the peppers.

# Cold Leek and Potato Soup

*Serve this flavourful soup with a dollop of crème fraîche or soured cream to add richness to this warming broth on cold winter evenings. Sprinkle with a few snipped fresh chives.*

*Serves 6–8*

450 g/1 lb potatoes, peeled and cubed

1.5 litres/2½ pints/6¼ cups vegetable stock

4 medium leeks, trimmed

150 ml/¼ pint/⅔ cup crème fraîche or
    soured cream

salt and freshly ground black pepper

45 ml/3 tbsp snipped fresh chives,
    to garnish

1 Put the potatoes and stock in a saucepan or flameproof casserole and bring to the boil. Reduce the heat and simmer for 15–20 minutes.

2 Make a slit along the length of each leek and rinse well under cold running water. Slice thinly.

3 When the potatoes are barely tender, stir in the leeks. Season with salt and pepper and simmer for 10–15 minutes until the vegetables are soft, stirring occasionally. If the soup appears too thick, thin it down with a little more of the stock or water.

4 Purée the soup in a blender or food processor, in batches if necessary. If you would prefer a very smooth soup, pass it through a food mill or press through a coarse sieve. Stir in most of the cream, cool and then chill. To serve, ladle into chilled bowls and garnish with a swirl of cream and snipped chives.

## VARIATION
❦

To make a low-fat soup, use low-fat fromage frais instead of crème fraîche or soured cream, or simply thin the soup with a little skimmed milk.

# Vegetable Korma

*The blending of spices produces a subtle, aromatic curry.*

INGREDIENTS

*Serves 4*

50 g/2 oz/4 tbsp butter

2 onions, sliced

2 garlic cloves, crushed

2.5 cm/1 in piece of fresh root
    ginger, grated

5 ml/1 tsp ground cumin

15 ml/1 tbsp ground coriander

6 cardamom pods

5 cm/2 in cinnamon stick

5 ml/1 tsp ground turmeric

1 fresh red chilli, seeded and
    finely chopped

1 potato, peeled and cut into 2.5 cm/
    1 in cubes

1 small aubergine, chopped

115 g/4 oz mushrooms, thickly sliced

115 g/4 oz/1 cup French beans, cut into
    2.5 cm/1 in lengths

60 ml/4 tbsp natural yogurt

150 ml/¼ pint/⅔ cup double cream

5 ml/1 tsp garam masala

salt and freshly ground black pepper

sprigs of fresh coriander, to garnish

poppadums, to serve

1 Melt the butter in a heavy-based saucepan. Add the onions and cook for 5 minutes, until soft. Add the garlic and ginger and cook for 2 minutes, then stir in the cumin, coriander, cardamoms, cinnamon stick, turmeric and chilli. Cook, stirring, for 30 seconds.

2 Add the potato, aubergine and mushrooms and about 175 ml/ 6 fl oz/¾ cup water. Cover the pan, bring to the boil, then lower the heat and simmer for 15 minutes. Add the beans and cook, uncovered, for 5 minutes.

### VARIATION
∽

Any combination of vegetables can be used for this korma, including carrots, cauliflower, broccoli, peas and chick-peas.

3 With a slotted spoon, remove the vegetables to a warmed serving dish and keep hot. Allow the cooking liquid to bubble up until it reduces a little. Season with salt and pepper, then stir in the yogurt, cream and garam masala. Pour the sauce over the vegetables and garnish with coriander. Serve with poppadums.

# Parmesan and Cauliflower Soup

*A silky smooth, mildly cheesy soup which isn't overpowered by the cauliflower. It makes an elegant dinner-party soup served with crisp Melba toast.*

## INGREDIENTS

*Serves 6*

1 large cauliflower
1.2 litres/2 pints/5 cups vegetable stock
   or water
175g/6oz farfalle
150ml/¼ pint/⅔ cup single cream or milk
freshly grated nutmeg
pinch of cayenne pepper
60ml/4 tbsp freshly grated
   Parmesan cheese
salt and ground black pepper

*For the Melba toast*
3–4 slices day-old white bread
freshly grated Parmesan cheese,
   for sprinkling
1.5ml/¼ tsp paprika

1 Cut the leaves and central stalk away from the cauliflower and discard. Divide the cauliflower into similar-size florets.

2 Bring the stock to the boil and add the cauliflower. Simmer for about 10 minutes or until very soft. Remove the cauliflower with a slotted spoon and place in a blender or food processor.

3 Add the pasta to the stock and simmer for 10 minutes until tender. Drain, reserve the pasta, and pour the liquid over the cauliflower. Add the cream or milk, nutmeg and cayenne to the cauliflower and blend until smooth.

4 Press the soup through a sieve then stir in the cooked pasta. Reheat the soup and stir in the Parmesan. Season to taste.

5 Meanwhile make the Melba toast. Preheat the oven to 180°C/350°F/Gas 4. Toast the bread lightly on both sides. Quickly cut off the crusts and split each slice in half horizontally. Scrape off any doughy bits and sprinkle with Parmesan and paprika. Place on a baking sheet and bake in the oven for about 10–15 minutes or until uniformly golden. Serve with the soup.

# Aubergine Curry

*A simple and delicious way of cooking aubergines, which retains their full flavour.*

*Serves 4*

2 large aubergines, about 450 g/1 lb each

45 ml/3 tbsp oil

2.5 ml/½ tsp black mustard seeds

1 bunch spring onions, finely chopped

115 g/4 oz button mushrooms, halved

2 garlic cloves, crushed

1 fresh red chilli, finely chopped

2.5 ml/½ tsp chilli powder

1 tsp ground cumin

1 tsp ground coriander

1.5 ml/¼ tsp ground turmeric

5 ml/1 tsp salt

400 g/14 oz can chopped tomatoes

15 ml/1 tbsp chopped fresh coriander

sprigs of fresh coriander, to garnish

1 Preheat the oven to 200°C/400°F/Gas 6. Brush both of the aubergines with 15 ml/1 tbsp of the oil and prick with a fork. Bake in the oven for 30–35 minutes, until the aubergines are soft.

2 Meanwhile, heat the remaining oil in a saucepan and fry the mustard seeds for 2 minutes, until they being to splutter.

3 Add the spring onions, mushrooms, garlic and chilli and fry for 5 minutes. Stir in the chilli powder, cumin, coriander, turmeric and salt and fry for 3–4 minutes. Add the tomatoes and simmer for 5 minutes.

4 Cut each of the aubergines in half lengthways and scoop out the soft flesh into a bowl. Mash the flesh briefly.

5 Add the mashed aubergine and fresh coriander to the saucepan. Bring to the boil and simmer for 5 minutes or until the sauce thickens. Serve garnished with coriander sprigs.

> ### COOK'S TIP
>
> If you want to omit some of the oil, wrap the aubergines in foil and bake in the oven for 1 hour.

# Italian Bean and Pasta Soup

*A thick and hearty soup which, followed by bread and cheese, makes a substantial lunch.*

INGREDIENTS

*Serves 6*

175g/6oz/1½ cups dried haricot beans, soaked overnight in cold water

1.75 litres/3 pints/7½ cups vegetable stock or water

115g/4oz medium pasta shells

60ml/4 tbsp olive oil, plus extra to serve

2 garlic cloves, crushed

60ml/4 tbsp chopped fresh parsley

salt and ground black pepper

1 Drain the beans and place in a large saucepan with the stock or water. Simmer, half-covered, for 2–2½ hours or until tender.

2 In a blender or food processor, process half the beans with a little of their cooking liquid, then stir into the unprocessed beans in the pan.

3 Add the pasta and simmer gently for 15 minutes until tender. (Add extra water or stock if the soup seems too thick.)

4 Heat the oil in a small pan and fry the garlic until golden. Stir into the soup with the parsley and season well with salt and pepper. Ladle into individual bowls and drizzle each with a little extra olive oil, to serve.

# Pizza with Fresh Vegetables

*This pizza can be made with any combination of fresh vegetables. Most will benefit from being blanched or sautéed before being baked on the pizza.*

*Serves 4*

400 g/14 oz peeled plum tomatoes, fresh or canned, weighed whole, without extra juice

2 medium broccoli spears

225 g/8 oz fresh asparagus

2 small courgettes

75 ml/5 tbsp olive oil

50 g/2 oz/⅓ cup shelled peas, fresh or frozen

4 spring onions, sliced

1 pizza base, 25–30 cm/10–12 in in diameter

75 g/3 oz/⅓ cup mozzarella cheese, cut into small dice

10 leaves fresh basil, torn into pieces

2 cloves garlic, finely chopped

salt and freshly ground black pepper

1 Preheat the oven to 240°C/475°F/Gas 9 for at least 20 minutes before baking the pizza. Strain the tomatoes through the medium hole of a food mill, scraping in all the pulp.

2 Peel the broccoli stems and asparagus, and blanch with the courgettes in a pan of boiling water for 4–5 minutes. Drain. Cut into bite-size pieces and slice the courgettes lengthways.

3 Heat 30 ml/2 tbsp of the olive oil in a small saucepan. Stir in the peas and spring onions and cook for 5–6 minutes, stirring often. Remove from the heat.

4 Spread the puréed tomatoes on to the pizza dough, leaving the rim uncovered. Add the other vegetables, spreading them evenly over the tomatoes.

5 Sprinkle with the mozzarella, basil, garlic, salt and pepper and remaining olive oil. Immediately place the pizza in the oven. Bake for about 20 minutes, or until the crust is golden brown and the cheese has melted.

# STARTERS

# Tagliatelle with Spinach Gnocchi

*Gnocchi are extremely smooth and light and make a delicious accompaniment to this pasta dish.*

INGREDIENTS

*Serves 4–6*

450 g/1 lb mixed flavoured tagliatelle
shavings of Parmesan cheese, to garnish

*For the spinach gnocchi*

450 g/1 lb frozen chopped spinach
1 small onion, finely chopped
1 garlic clove, crushed
1.5 ml/¼ tsp ground nutmeg
400 g/14 oz low-fat cottage cheese
115 g/4 oz dried white breadcrumbs
75 g/3 oz semolina or plain flour
50 g/2 oz grated Parmesan cheese
3 egg whites

*For the tomato sauce*

1 onion, finely chopped
1 stick celery, finely chopped
1 red pepper, seeded and diced
1 garlic clove, crushed
150 ml/¼ pint/⅔ cup vegetable stock
400 g/14 oz can tomatoes
15 ml/1 tbsp tomato purée
10 ml/2 tsp caster sugar
5 ml/1 tsp dried oregano
salt and freshly ground black pepper

1 To make the tomato sauce, put the chopped onion, celery, pepper and garlic into a non-stick pan. Add the stock, bring to the boil and cook for 5 minutes or until tender.

2 Add the tomatoes, tomato purée, sugar and oregano. Season to taste, bring to the boil and simmer for 30 minutes until thick, stirring occasionally.

3 Put the spinach, onion and garlic into a saucepan, cover and cook until the spinach is defrosted. Remove the lid and increase the heat. Season with salt, pepper and nutmeg. Cool in a bowl. Mix in the remaining ingredients. Shape into about 24 ovals and refrigerate for 30 minutes.

4 Cook the gnocchi in boiling salted water for about 5 minutes. Remove with a slotted spoon and drain. Cook the tagliatelle in a pan of boiling salted water until *al dente*. Drain. Transfer to serving plates, top with gnocchi, the tomato sauce and shavings of Parmesan cheese.

# Guacamole

*This is quite a fiery version, although nowhere near as hot as you would be served in Mexico!*

INGREDIENTS

*Serves 4*

2 ripe avocados, peeled and stoned

2 tomatoes, peeled, seeded and finely chopped

6 spring onions, finely chopped

1–2 fresh chillies, seeded and finely chopped

30 ml/2 tbsp fresh lime or lemon juice

15 ml/1 tbsp chopped fresh coriander

salt and freshly ground black pepper

coriander sprigs, to garnish

1 Put the avocado halves into a large bowl and mash them roughly with a large fork.

2 Add the remaining ingredients. Mix well and season with salt and pepper. Serve garnished with fresh coriander.

# Harvest Vegetable and Lentil Casserole

*Take advantage of root vegetables in season to produce a hearty dish that's not only full of natural goodness but delicious too.*

INGREDIENTS

*Serves 6*

15 ml/1 tbsp sunflower oil

2 leeks, sliced

1 garlic clove, crushed

4 celery sticks, chopped

2 carrots, sliced

2 parsnips, diced

1 sweet potato, diced

225 g/8 oz swede, diced

175 g/6 oz whole brown or green lentils

450 g/1 lb tomatoes, skinned, seeded and chopped

15 ml/1 tbsp chopped fresh thyme

15 ml/1 tbsp chopped fresh marjoram

900 ml/1½ pints/3¾ cups vegetable stock

15 ml/1 tbsp cornflour

salt and freshly ground black pepper

sprigs of fresh thyme, to garnish

1 Preheat the oven to 180°C/350°F/Gas 4. Heat the oil in a flameproof casserole over moderate heat. Add the leeks, garlic and celery and cook gently for 3 minutes.

2 Add the carrots, parsnips, sweet potato, swede, lentils, tomatoes, herbs, stock and seasoning. Stir well. Bring to the boil, stirring occasionally.

3 Cover and bake in the oven for about 50 minutes, until the vegetables and the lentils are cooked and tender. While it is cooking, remove the casserole from the oven and stir the vegetable mixture once or twice so that it is evenly cooked.

4 Remove the casserole from the oven. Blend the cornflour with 45 ml/3 tbsp water in a bowl. Stir into the casserole and heat, stirring continuously, until the mixture comes to the boil and thickens. Simmer gently for 2 minutes.

5 Spoon the vegetable mixture into bowls and serve garnished with thyme sprigs.

# Butter Bean, Watercress and Herb Dip

*This is a refreshing dip that is especially good served with fresh vegetable crudités and breadsticks.*

*Serves 4–6*

225 g/8 oz/1 cup plain cottage cheese

400 g/14 oz can butter beans, rinsed and drained

1 bunch spring onions, chopped

50 g/2 oz watercress, chopped

60 ml/4 tbsp mayonnaise

45 ml/3 tbsp chopped fresh mixed herbs

salt and freshly ground black pepper

watercress sprigs, to garnish

vegetable crudités and breadsticks, to serve

1 Put the cottage cheese, butter beans, spring onions, watercress, mayonnaise and herbs in a blender or food processor and blend until fairly smooth.

2 Season with salt and pepper and spoon the mixture into a dish.

3 Cover and chill for several hours before serving.

4 Transfer to a serving dish (or individual dishes) and garnish with watercress sprigs. Serve with vegetable crudités and breadsticks.

COOK'S TIP

Try using other canned beans such as cannellini beans or chick-peas in place of the butter beans.

# Purée of Lentils with Baked Eggs

*This unusual dish makes an excellent supper. For a nutty flavour you could add a 400 g/14 oz can of unsweetened chestnut purée to the lentil mixture.*

INGREDIENTS

*Serves 4*

450 g/1 lb/2 cups washed brown lentils

3 leeks, thinly sliced

10 ml/2 tsp coriander seeds, crushed

15 ml/1 tbsp chopped fresh coriander

30 ml/2 tbsp chopped fresh mint

15 ml/1 tbsp red wine vinegar

1 litre/1¾ pints/4 cups vegetable stock

4 eggs

salt and freshly ground black pepper

generous handful of fresh parsley, chopped, to garnish

1 Put the lentils in a deep saucepan. Add the leeks, coriander seeds, fresh coriander, mint, vinegar and stock. Bring to the boil, then lower the heat and simmer for 30–40 minutes, until the lentils are cooked and have absorbed all the liquid.

2 Preheat the oven to 180°C/350°F/Gas 4.

3 Season the lentils with salt and pepper and mix well. Spread out in four lightly greased baking dishes.

4 Using the back of a spoon, make a hollow in the lentil mixture in each dish. Break an egg into each hollow. Cover the dishes with foil and bake for 15–20 minutes, or until the egg whites are set and the yolks are still soft. Sprinkle with plenty of parsley and serve at once.

# Saffron Dip

*Serve this mild dip with fresh vegetable crudités – it is particularly good with florets of cauliflower.*

INGREDIENTS

*Serves 4*

small pinch of saffron strands
200 g/7 oz fromage frais
10 fresh chives
10 fresh basil leaves
salt and freshly ground black pepper
vegetable crudités, to serve

1 Pour 15 ml/1 tbsp boiling water into a small heatproof bowl and add the saffron strands. Leave to infuse for about 3–4 minutes, stirring occasionally.

2 Beat the fromage frais until smooth, then stir in the infused saffron liquid.

3 Use a pair of scissors to snip the chives into the dip. Tear the basil leaves into small pieces and stir them in.

4 Season with salt and pepper. Serve immediately with vegetable crudités.

## VARIATION

Leave out the saffron and add a squeeze of lemon or lime juice instead. Alternatively, substitute the saffron strands with ready-ground saffron powder.

# Butternut Squash and Sage Pizza

*The combination of sweet butternut squash, sage and sharp goat's cheese works wonderfully on this pizza.*

INGREDIENTS

*Serves 4*

2.5 ml/½ tsp active dried yeast

pinch of granulated sugar

450 g/1 lb/4 cups strong white flour

5 ml/1 tsp salt

30 ml/2 tbsp olive oil

15 g/½ oz/1 tbsp butter

30 ml/2 tbsp olive oil

2 shallots, finely chopped

1 butternut squash, peeled, seeded and
  cubed, about 450 g/1 lb prepared weight

16 sage leaves

2 x 400 g/14 oz cans fresh tomato sauce

115 g/4 oz/1 cup mozzarella cheese, sliced

115 g/4 oz/½ cup firm goat's cheese

salt and freshly ground black pepper

1 Put 300 ml/½ pint/1¼ cups warm water in a measuring jug. Add the yeast and sugar and leave for 5–10 minutes, until it is frothy.

2 Sift the flour and salt into a large bowl and make a well in the centre. Gradually pour in the yeast mixture and the olive oil. Mix to make a smooth dough. Knead on a lightly floured surface for about 10 minutes until smooth, springy and elastic. Place the dough in a floured bowl, cover and leave to rise in a warm place for 1½ hours.

3 Preheat the oven to 200°C/400°F/Gas 6. Oil four baking sheets. Put the butter and oil in a roasting tin and heat in the oven for a few minutes. Add the shallots, squash and half the sage leaves. Toss to coat. Roast for 15–20 minutes, until tender.

4 Raise the oven temperature to 220°C/425°F/Gas 7. Divide the dough into four equal pieces and roll out each piece on a floured surface to a 25 cm/10 in round.

5 Transfer each round to a baking sheet and spread with tomato sauce, leaving a 1 cm/½ in border all around. Spoon the squash and shallot mixture over the top.

6 Arrange the mozzarella over the squash mixture and crumble the goat's cheese over. Scatter the remaining sage leaves over and season with plenty of salt and pepper. Bake for 15–20 minutes, until the cheese has melted and the crusts are golden.

# Spiced Carrot Dip

*This is a delicious dip with a sweet and spicy flavour. Serve wheat crackers or fiery tortilla chips as accompaniments for dipping.*

*Serves 4*

1 onion

3 carrots, plus extra to garnish

grated rind and juice of 2 oranges

15 ml/1 tbsp hot curry paste

150 ml/¼ pint/⅔ cup natural yogurt

handful of fresh basil leaves

15–30 ml/1–2 tbsp fresh lemon juice, to taste

red Tabasco sauce, to taste

salt and freshly ground black pepper

3 Stir in the yogurt, then tear the basil leaves roughly into small pieces and stir them into the carrot mixture.

4 Add the lemon juice and Tabasco and season with salt and pepper. Serve within a few hours at room temperature. Garnish with grated carrot.

1 Finely chop the onion. Peel and grate the carrots. Place the onion, carrots, orange rind and juice, and curry paste in a small saucepan. Bring to the boil, cover and simmer gently for 10 minutes, until tender.

2 Process the mixture in a blender or food processor until smooth. Leave to cool completely.

# Spiced Tofu Stir-fry

*The colours in this aromatic stir-fry are as pleasing to the eye as the flavours are to the palate. Serve with noodles or egg-fried rice.*

*Serves 4*

10 ml/2 tsp ground cumin

15 ml/1 tbsp paprika

5 ml/1 tsp ground ginger

good pinch of cayenne pepper

15 ml/1 tbsp caster sugar

275 g/10 oz tofu (beancurd)

60 ml/4 tbsp oil

2 garlic cloves, crushed

1 bunch spring onions, sliced

1 red pepper, seeded and sliced

1 yellow pepper, seeded and sliced

225g/8 oz/generous 3 cups brown-cap
   mushrooms, halved or quartered
   if necessary

1 large courgette, sliced

115 g/4 oz fine green beans, halved

50 g/2 oz/scant ½ cup pine nuts

15 ml/1 tbsp lime juice

15ml/1 tbsp clear honey

salt and pepper

1 Mix together the cumin, paprika, ginger, cayenne and sugar with plenty of seasoning. Cut the tofu into cubes and coat them in the spice mixture.

2 Heat some of the oil in a wok or large frying pan. Cook the tofu over a high heat for 3–4 minutes, turning occasionally (take care not to break up the tofu too much). Remove with a slotted spoon. Wipe out the pan with kitchen paper.

3 Add the remaining oil to the pan and cook the garlic and spring onions for 3 minutes. Add the remaining vegetables and cook over a medium heat for 6 minutes, or until beginning to soften and turn golden. Season well.

4 Return the tofu to the pan with the pine nuts, lime juice and honey. Heat through and serve immediately.

# Aubergine Dip with Crispy Bread

*This delectable Middle Eastern dish is flavoured with tahini (sesame seed paste), which gives it a subtle hint of spice.*

*Serves 6*

2 small aubergines

1 garlic clove, crushed

60 ml/4 tbsp tahini (sesame seed paste)

25 g/1 oz/¼ cup ground almonds

juice of ½ lemon

2.5 ml/½ tsp ground cumin

30 ml/2 tbsp fresh mint leaves

30 ml/2 tbsp olive oil

salt and freshly ground black pepper

*Lebanese flatbread*

4 pitta breads

45 ml/3 tbsp toasted sesame seeds

45 ml/3 tbsp fresh thyme leaves, chopped

45 ml/3 tbsp poppy seeds

150 ml/¼ pint/⅔ cup olive oil

3 Grill the aubergines, turning them frequently, until the skin is blackened and blistered. Remove the skin, chop the flesh roughly and leave to drain in a colander. Wait for 30 minutes, then squeeze out as much liquid from the aubergines as possible.

4 Place the flesh in a blender or food processor. Add the garlic, tahini, almonds, lemon juice and cumin. Season, and process to a smooth paste. Chop half the mint and stir in.

5 Spoon into a bowl, scatter the remaining mint leaves on top and drizzle with olive oil. Serve with the Lebanese flatbread.

1 Start by making the Lebanese flatbread. Split the pitta breads through the middle and carefully open them out. Mix the sesame seeds, chopped thyme and poppy seeds in a mortar. Crush them lightly with a pestle to release the flavour.

2 Stir in the olive oil. Spread the mixture lightly over the cut sides of the pitta bread. Grill until golden brown and crisp. When completely cool, break into pieces and set aside.

# Vegetable Chilli

*This alternative to traditional chilli con carne is delicious served with brown rice.*

*Serves 4*

2 onions, chopped

1 garlic clove, crushed

3 sticks celery, chopped

1 green pepper, seeded and diced

225 g/8 oz mushrooms, sliced

2 courgettes, sliced

400 g/14 oz can red kidney beans, rinsed and drained

400 g/14 oz can chopped tomatoes

150 ml/¼ pint/⅔ cup passata

30 ml/2 tbsp tomato purée

15 ml/1 tbsp tomato ketchup

1 tsp each hot chilli powder, ground cumin and ground coriander

salt and freshly ground black pepper

natural yogurt and cayenne pepper, to serve

sprigs of fresh coriander, to garnish

1 Put the onions, garlic, celery, green pepper, mushrooms and courgettes in a large saucepan and mix together.

2 Add the kidney beans, tomatoes, passata, tomato purée and tomato ketchup.

3 Add the spices, season with salt and pepper and mix well.

4 Cover, bring to the boil and simmer for 20–30 minutes, stirring occasionally, until the vegetables are tender. Serve with natural yogurt, sprinkled with cayenne pepper. Garnish with fresh coriander sprigs.

# Chick-pea Falafel with Coriander Dip

*Little balls of spicy chick-pea purée, deep-fried until crisp, are served with a zesty coriander-flavoured mayonnaise.*

### INGREDIENTS

*Serves 4*

400 g/14 oz can chick-peas, drained
6 spring onions, finely chopped
1 egg
2.5 ml/½ tsp ground turmeric
1 garlic clove, crushed
5 ml/1 tsp ground cumin
60 ml/4 tbsp chopped fresh coriander
oil for deep-frying
1 small fresh red chilli, seeded and
　　finely chopped
45 ml/3 tbsp mayonnaise
salt and freshly ground black pepper
sprig of fresh coriander, to garnish

1 Put the chick-peas into a food processor or blender. Add the spring onions and process to a smooth purée. Add the egg, ground turmeric, garlic, cumin and about 15 ml/1 tbsp of the chopped coriander. Process briefly to mix, then season with salt and pepper.

2 Working with clean, wet hands, shape the chick-pea mixture into about 16 small balls.

3 Heat the oil for deep-frying to 180°C/350°F or until a cube of bread, when added to the oil, browns in 30–45 seconds. Deep-fry the falafel in batches for 2–3 minutes or until golden. Drain the falafel on kitchen paper. Place in a serving bowl and keep warm.

4 Stir the remaining chopped coriander and the chilli into the mayonnaise. Garnish with the coriander sprig and serve alongside the falafel.

# Risotto alla Milanese

*This traditional Italian risotto is rich and creamy, and deliciously flavoured with garlic, shavings of Parmesan and fresh parsley.*

*Serves 4*

2 garlic cloves, crushed
60 ml/4 tbsp chopped fresh parsley
finely grated rind of 1 lemon

*For the risotto*

5 ml/1 tsp (or 1 sachet) saffron strands
25 g/1 oz/2 tbsp butter
1 large onion, finely chopped
275 g/10 oz/1½ cups arborio rice
150 ml/¼ pint/⅔ cup dry white wine
1 litre/1¾ pints/4 cups vegetable stock
Parmesan cheese shavings, to serve
salt and freshly ground black pepper

1 Mix together the garlic, parsley and lemon rind in a bowl. Reserve and set aside.

2 To make the risotto, put the saffron in a small bowl with 15 ml/1 tbsp boiling water and leave to stand while the saffron is infused. Melt the butter in a heavy-based frying saucepan and gently fry the onion for 5 minutes, until softened and golden.

3 Stir in the rice and cook for about 2 minutes until it becomes translucent. Add the wine and saffron mixture and cook for several minutes until all the wine is absorbed.

4 Add 600 ml/1 pint/2½ cups of the stock to the pan and simmer gently until the stock is absorbed, stirring frequently.

5 Gradually add more stock, a ladleful at a time, until the rice is tender. (The rice might be tender and creamy before you've added all the stock, so add it slowly towards the end of the cooking time.)

6 Season the risotto with salt and pepper and transfer to a serving dish. Scatter lavishly with shavings of Parmesan cheese and the garlic and parsley mixture.

# Marinated Vegetable Antipasto

*This colourful selection of fresh vegetables and herbs makes a great starter when served with fresh crusty bread.*

*Serves 4*

*For the peppers*

3 red peppers

3 yellow peppers

4 garlic cloves, sliced

handful of fresh basil

120 ml/4 fl oz/½ cup olive oil

salt and freshly ground black pepper

*For the mushrooms*

450 g/1 lb open cap mushrooms, thickly sliced

60 ml/4 tbsp olive oil

1 large garlic clove, crushed

15 ml/1 tbsp chopped fresh rosemary

250 ml/8 fl oz/1 cup dry white wine

fresh rosemary sprigs, to garnish

*For the olives*

1 dried red chilli, crushed

grated rind of 1 lemon

120 ml/4 fl oz/½ cup olive oil

225 g/8 oz/1⅓ cups Italian black olives

30 ml/2 tbsp chopped fresh flat leaf parsley

basil leaves, to garnish

1 lemon wedge, to serve

1 Place the peppers under a hot grill. Cook until they are black and blistered all over. Remove from the heat and place in a large plastic bag to cool.

2 When the peppers are cool, remove their skins, halve the flesh and remove the seeds. Cut into strips lengthways and place them in a bowl with the sliced garlic and basil leaves. Season and then cover with oil and marinate for 3–4 hours, tossing occasionally. Garnish with basil leaves.

3 Place the mushrooms in a large bowl. Heat the oil in a pan and add the garlic, rosemary and wine. Bring to the boil, then simmer for 3 minutes. Season. Pour over the mushrooms.

4 Mix well and leave to cool, stirring occasionally. Cover and marinate overnight. Serve at room temperature, garnished with rosemary sprigs.

5 Place the chilli and lemon rind in a small pan with the oil. Heat gently for about 3 minutes. Add the olives and heat for 1 minute more. Tip the olive mixture into a bowl and leave to cool. Marinate overnight. Before serving, sprinkle with parsley and garnish with basil leaves. Serve with the lemon wedge.

# Red Pepper Risotto

The character of this delicious risotto depends on the type of rice you use. With arborio rice, the risotto should be moist and creamy. If you use brown rice, reduce the amount of liquid for a drier dish with a nutty flavour.

## INGREDIENTS

Serves 6

3 large red peppers

30 ml/2 tbsp olive oil

3 large garlic cloves, thinly sliced

1½ x 400 g/14 oz cans chopped tomatoes

2 bay leaves

1.2–1.5 litres/2–2½ pints/5–6¼ cups
   vegetable stock

450 g/1 lb/2½ cups arborio rice or
   brown rice

6 fresh basil leaves, snipped

salt and freshly ground black pepper

1 Preheat the grill. Put the peppers in a grill pan and grill until the skins are blackened and blistered all over. Put the peppers in a bowl, cover with several layers of damp kitchen paper and leave for 10 minutes. Peel off the skins, then slice the peppers, discarding the cores and seeds.

2 Heat the oil in a wide, shallow pan. Add the garlic and tomatoes and cook over a gentle heat for 5 minutes, then add the pepper slices and bay leaves. Stir well and cook for 15 minutes more, still over a gentle heat.

3 Pour the stock into a large, heavy-based saucepan and heat it to simmering point. Stir the rice into the vegetable mixture and cook for about 2 minutes, then add two or three ladlefuls of the hot stock. Cook, stirring occasionally, until all the stock has been absorbed into the rice.

4 Continue to add stock in this way, making sure each addition has been absorbed before pouring in the next. When the rice is tender, season with salt and pepper. Remove the pan from the heat, cover and leave to stand for 10 minutes before stirring in the basil and serving.

# Spicy Potato Wedges with Chilli Dip

*The spicy crust on these potato wedges makes them irresistible, especially when served with a zesty chilli dip.*

*Serves 2*

2 baking potatoes, about 225 g/8 oz each

30 ml/2 tbsp olive oil

2 garlic cloves, crushed

5 ml/1 tsp ground allspice

5 ml/1 tsp ground coriander

15 ml/1 tbsp paprika

salt and freshly ground black pepper

*For the dip*

15 ml/1 tbsp olive oil

1 small onion, finely chopped

1 garlic clove, crushed

200 g/7 oz can chopped tomatoes

1 fresh red chilli, seeded and
　finely chopped

15 ml/1 tbsp balsamic vinegar

15 ml/1 tbsp chopped fresh coriander,
　plus extra to garnish

1 Preheat the oven to 200°C/400°F/Gas 6. Wash the potatoes, cut in half, then into 8 wedges.

2 Place the potato wedges in a saucepan of cold water. Bring to the boil, then lower the heat and simmer gently for 10 minutes, or until the potatoes have softened slightly. Drain well and pat dry on kitchen paper.

3 Mix the oil, garlic, allspice, coriander and paprika in a roasting tin. Season with salt and pepper. Add the potatoes and shake to coat thoroughly. Roast for 20 minutes, turning occasionally.

4 Meanwhile, make the chilli dip. Heat the oil in a saucepan, add the onion and garlic and cook for 5–10 minutes until soft and golden. Add the tomatoes with their juice and stir in the chilli and vinegar.

5 Cook gently for 10 minutes, until the mixture has reduced and thickened. Season with salt and pepper. Stir in the fresh coriander and serve hot, with the potato wedges. Garnish with salt, freshly ground black pepper and fresh coriander.

# Vegetable Pilau

*A popular vegetable rice dish that makes a tasty light supper.*

## INGREDIENTS

*Serves 4–6*

225 g/8 oz/1 cup basmati rice
30 ml/2 tbsp oil
2.5 ml/½ tsp cumin seeds
2 bay leaves
4 green cardamom pods
4 cloves
1 onion, finely chopped
1 carrot, finely diced
50 g/2 oz/⅓ cup frozen peas, thawed
50 g/2 oz/⅓ cup frozen sweetcorn, thawed
25 g/1 oz/¼ cup cashew nuts, lightly fried
1.5 ml/¼ tsp ground cumin
salt

1 Wash the basmati rice in several changes of cold water. Put into a bowl and cover with water. Leave to soak for about 30 minutes.

2 Heat the oil in a large frying pan and fry the cumin seeds for 2 minutes. Add the bay leaves, cardamoms and cloves and fry for a further 2 minutes.

3 Add the onion and fry for 5 minutes, until softened and lightly browned.

4 Stir in the carrot and cook for 3–4 minutes.

5 Drain the rice and add to the pan together with the peas, sweetcorn and cashew nuts. Fry for 4–5 minutes.

6 Add 475 ml/16 fl oz/2 cups water, ground cumin and salt. Bring to the boil, cover and simmer for 15 minutes over a low heat until all the water is absorbed. Leave to stand, covered, for 10 minutes, before serving.

# Potted Stilton with Herbs and Melba Toast

*This starter is a great time saver, as the potted Stilton can be made the day before, and the Melba toast will keep in an airtight container for up to two days.*

*Serves 8*

225 g/8 oz/1 cup blue Stilton or other
    blue cheese
115 g/4 oz/½ cup cream cheese
15 ml/1 tbsp port
15 ml/1 tbsp chopped fresh parsley
15 ml/1 tbsp snipped fresh chives, plus
    extra to garnish
50 g/2 oz/½ cup finely chopped walnuts
salt and freshly ground black pepper

*For the Melba toast*
12 thin slices of white bread

1 Put the Stilton or blue cheese, cream cheese and port into a blender or food processor and process until smooth.

2 Stir in the remaining ingredients and then season with salt and pepper.

3 Spoon into individual ramekin dishes and level the tops. Cover with clear film and chill until firm. Sprinkle with snipped chives just before serving.

4 To make the Melba toast, preheat the oven to 180°C/350°F/Gas 4. Toast the bread on both sides.

5 While the toast is still hot, cut off the crusts and cut each slice horizontally in two. While the bread is still warm, place it in a single layer on baking trays and bake for 10–15 minutes, until golden brown and crisp. Continue with the remaining slices in the same way. Serve warm with the potted Stilton.

# SUPPERS

# Mushroom and Bean Pâté

*A light and tasty pâté, delicious
served on wholemeal bread or toast.*

INGREDIENTS

*Serves 12*

450 g/1 lb mushrooms, sliced

1 onion, chopped

2 garlic cloves, crushed

1 red pepper, seeded and diced

30 ml/2 tbsp vegetable stock

30 ml/2 tbsp dry white wine

400 g/14 oz can red kidney beans, rinsed
    and drained

1 egg, beaten

50 g/2 oz/1 cup fresh wholemeal
    breadcrumbs

15 ml/1 tbsp chopped fresh thyme

15 ml/1 tbsp chopped fresh rosemary

salt and freshly ground black pepper

lettuce and tomatoes, to garnish

1 Preheat the oven to
180°C/350°F/Gas 4. Lightly
grease and line a non-stick 900 g/
2 lb loaf tin. Put the mushrooms,
onion, garlic, red pepper, stock and
wine in a saucepan. Cover and
cook for about 10 minutes, stirring
occasionally.

2 Set aside to cool slightly, then
purée the mixture with the
kidney beans in a blender or food
processor until smooth.

3 Transfer the mixture to a bowl,
add the egg, breadcrumbs and
herbs and mix thoroughly. Season
with salt and pepper.

4 Spoon the mixture into the
prepared tin and level the
surface. Bake for 45–60 minutes,
until lightly set and browned on
top. Place on a wire rack and allow
the pâté to cool completely in the
tin. Once cool, cover and refrigerate for several hours. Turn out of
the tin and serve in slices,
garnished with lettuce and tomato.

# Mushroom Picker's Omelette

*Perfect for Sunday brunch, this omelette is simplicity itself to make.*

## INGREDIENTS

*Serves 1*

25 g/1 oz/2 tbsp unsalted butter, plus extra
  for cooking
115 g/4 oz assorted wild and cultivated
  mushrooms such as young ceps, bay
  boletus, chanterelles, saffron milk-caps,
  closed field mushrooms, oyster
  mushrooms, hedgehog and St George's
  mushrooms, trimmed and sliced
3 eggs, at room temperature
salt and freshly ground black pepper

1 Melt the butter in a small omelette pan, add the mushrooms and cook until the juices run. Season with salt and pepper, remove from pan and set aside. Wipe the pan.

2 Break the eggs into a bowl, season and beat with a fork. Heat the pan over high heat, add a knob of butter and let it begin to brown. Pour in the beaten egg and stir briskly with the back of a fork.

3 When the eggs are two-thirds set, add the mushrooms and let the omelette finish cooking for 10–15 seconds.

4 Tap the handle of the omelette pan sharply with your fist to loosen the omelette from the pan, then fold and turn on to a plate. Serve with warm crusty bread and a simple green salad.

# Garlic Mushrooms with a Parsley Crust

*These garlic mushrooms are perfect for dinner parties, or you could serve them in larger portions as a light supper dish with a green salad.*

INGREDIENTS

*Serves 4*

350 g/12 oz large mushrooms, stems removed

3 garlic cloves, crushed

175 g/6 oz/¾ cup butter, softened ·

50 g/2 oz/1 cup fresh white breadcrumbs

50 g/2 oz/1 cup fresh parsley, chopped

1 egg, beaten

salt and cayenne pepper

8 cherry tomatoes, to garnish

1 Preheat the oven to 190°C/375°F/Gas 5. Arrange the mushrooms cup side uppermost on a baking tray. Mix together the garlic and butter in a small bowl and divide 115 g/4 oz/ ½ cup of the butter between all the mushrooms.

2 Heat the remaining butter in a frying pan and lightly fry the breadcrumbs until golden brown. Place the chopped parsley in a bowl, add the breadcrumbs, season with salt and cayenne pepper and mix well.

3 Stir in the egg and use the mixture to fill the mushroom caps. Bake for 10–15 minutes until the topping has browned and the mushrooms have softened. Garnish with quartered tomatoes.

### COOK'S TIP

If you are planning ahead, stuffed mushrooms can be prepared up to 12 hours in advance and kept in the fridge before baking.

# Omelette with Beans

*Every good cook should have a few omelettes in their repertoire. This version includes soft white beans and is finished with a layer of toasted sesame seeds.*

INGREDIENTS

*Serves 4*

30 ml/2 tbsp olive oil

5 ml/1 tsp sesame oil

1 Spanish onion, chopped

1 small red pepper, seeded and diced

2 celery sticks, chopped

1 x 400 g/14 oz can soft white
   beans, drained

8 eggs

45 ml/3 tbsp sesame seeds

salt and freshly ground black pepper

green salad, to serve

3 In a small bowl, beat the eggs with a fork, season with salt and pepper and pour over the ingredients in the pan.

4 Stir the egg mixture with a flat wooden spoon until it begins to stiffen, then allow to firm over a low heat for 6-8 minutes.

5 Preheat a moderate grill. Sprinkle the omelette with sesame seeds and brown evenly under the grill.

6 Cut the omelette into thick wedges and serve warm with a green salad.

1 Heat the olive and sesame oils in a 30 cm/12 in flameproof frying pan. Add the onion, pepper and celery and cook to soften without colouring.

2 Add the beans and continue to cook for several minutes to heat through.

## VARIATION

You can also use sliced cooked potatoes, any seasonal vegetables, baby artichoke hearts and chick-peas in this omelette.

# Asparagus Rolls with Herb Butter Sauce

*For a taste sensation, try tender
asparagus spears wrapped in crisp
filo pastry. The buttery herb sauce
makes the perfect accompaniment.*

## INGREDIENTS

*Serves 2*

4 sheets of filo pastry

50 g/2 oz/¼ cup butter, melted

16 young asparagus spears, trimmed

*For the sauce*

2 shallots, finely chopped

1 bay leaf

150 ml/¼ pint/⅔ cup dry white wine

175 g/6 oz butter, softened

15 ml/1 tbsp chopped fresh herbs

salt and freshly ground black pepper

chopped chives, to garnish

1 Preheat the oven to
200°C/400°F/Gas 6. Cut the filo
sheets in half. Brush a half sheet
with melted butter. Fold one
corner of the sheet down to the
bottom edge to give a wedge shape.

2 Lay 4 asparagus spears on top
at the longest edge, and roll up
toward the shortest edge. Using the
remaining filo and asparagus
spears, make three more rolls in
the same way.

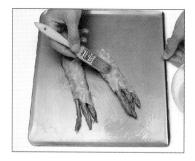

3 Lay the rolls on a greased
baking sheet. Brush with the
remaining melted butter. Bake in
the oven for 8 minutes until
golden brown.

4 Meanwhile, put the shallots,
bay leaf and wine into a pan.
Cover, and cook over a high heat
until the wine is reduced to 45–60
ml/3–4 tbsp.

5 Strain the wine mixture into a
bowl. Whisk in the butter, a
little at a time until the sauce is
smooth and glossy.

6 Stir in the herbs and add salt
and pepper to taste. Return to
the pan and keep the sauce warm.
Serve the rolls on individual plates
with a salad garnish, if desired.
Serve the sauce separately,
sprinkled with a scattering of
chopped chives.

# Sun-dried Tomato and Parmesan Carbonara

*Ingredients for this recipe can easily be doubled up to serve four. Why not try it with plenty of garlic bread and a big green salad?*

*Serves 2*

175 g/6 oz tagliatelle

50 g/2 oz sun-dried tomatoes in olive oil, drained

2 eggs, beaten

150 ml/¼ pint/⅔ cup double cream

15 ml/1 tbsp wholegrain mustard

50 g/2 oz/⅔ cup Parmesan cheese, freshly grated

12 fresh basil leaves, shredded

salt and pepper

fresh basil leaves, to garnish

crusty bread, to serve

1 Cook the pasta in boiling, salted water until it is just tender but still retains a little bite (*al dente*).

2 Meanwhile, cut the sun-dried tomatoes into small pieces.

3 Beat together the eggs, cream and mustard in a bowl. Add plenty of salt and pepper until they are well combined and smooth but do not allow the mixture to become frothy.

4 Drain the pasta and immediately return to the hot saucepan with the cream mixture, sun-dried tomatoes, Parmesan cheese and shredded fresh basil. Return to a very low heat for 1 minute, stirring gently until the mixture thickens slightly. Adjust the seasoning and serve immediately, garnished with basil leaves. Serve with plenty of crusty bread.

# Fried Mozzarella

*These crispy cheese slices make an unusual and tasty starter. They must be cooked just before serving.*

INGREDIENTS

*Serves 2–3*

300 g/11 oz/1¾ cups mozzarella cheese

oil for deep frying

2 eggs

flour seasoned with salt and freshly
   ground black pepper

plain dry breadcrumbs

flat leaf parsley, to garnish

1 Cut the mozzarella into slices about 1 cm/½ in thick. Gently pat off any excess moisture with kitchen paper.

2 Heat the oil to 185°C/360°F or until a small piece of bread sizzles as soon as it is dropped in. While the oil is heating, beat the eggs in a shallow bowl. Spread some seasoned flour on one plate and some breadcrumbs on another.

3 Press the cheese slices into the flour, coating them evenly with a thin layer of flour. Shake off any excess. Dip them into the egg, then once into the breadcrumbs. Dip them once more into the egg, then again into the breadcrumbs.

4 Fry immediately in the hot oil until golden brown. (You may have to do this in two batches but do not let the breaded cheese wait for too long or the breadcrumb coating will separate from the cheese while it is being fried.) Drain on kitchen paper and serve hot, garnished with parsley.

# Fresh Ceps with a Parsley Dressing

*To capture the just-picked flavour of mushrooms, try this delicious salad enriched with an egg yolk and walnut oil dressing. Choose small ceps or bay boletus for a firm texture and a fine flavour.*

*Serves 4*

350 g/12 oz fresh ceps or bay boletus

175 g/6 oz mixed salad leaves such as bativia, young spinach and frisée

50 g/2 oz/½ cup broken walnut pieces, toasted

50 g/2 oz Parmesan cheese

salt and freshly ground black pepper

*For the dressing*

2 egg yolks

2.5 ml/½ tsp French mustard

75 ml/5 tbsp groundnut oil

45 ml/3 tbsp walnut oil

30 ml/2 tbsp lemon juice

30 ml/2 tbsp chopped fresh parsley

pinch of caster sugar

1 For the dressing, place the egg yolks in a screw-top jar with the mustard, oils, lemon juice, parsley and sugar. Shake well.

2 Slice the mushrooms thinly using a sharp knife.

3 Place the mushrooms in a large salad bowl and combine with the dressing. Leave to stand for 10–15 minutes for the flavours to mingle.

4 Wash and spin the salad leaves, then toss with the mushrooms.

5 Turn out on to four large plates, season with salt and pepper then scatter with toasted walnut pieces and shavings of Parmesan cheese.

## COOK'S TIP

The dressing for this salad uses raw egg yolks. Be sure to use only the freshest eggs from a reputable supplier. Pregnant women, young children and the elderly are not advised to eat raw egg yolks. If this presents a problem, the dressing can be made without the egg yolks.

# Greek Cheese and Potato Patties

*Delicious little fried morsels of potato and feta cheese, flavoured with dill and lemon juice.*

### INGREDIENTS

*Serves 4*

500 g/1¼ lb potatoes

115 g/4 oz feta cheese

4 spring onions, chopped

45 ml/3 tbsp chopped fresh dill

15 ml/1 tbsp lemon juice

1 egg, beaten

flour for dredging

45 ml/3 tbsp olive oil

salt and freshly ground black pepper

1 Boil the potatoes in their skins in lightly salted water until soft. Drain, then peel while still warm. Place in a bowl and mash. Crumble the feta cheese into the potatoes and add the spring onions, dill, lemon juice and egg. Season with salt and pepper (the cheese is salty, so taste before you add salt). Stir well.

2 Cover the mixture and chill until firm. Divide the mixture into walnut-size balls, then flatten them slightly. Dredge with the flour. Heat the oil in a frying pan and fry the patties until golden brown on each side. Drain on kitchen paper and serve at once.

# Sweetcorn Cakes with Grilled Tomatoes

*Crisp sweetcorn fritters are simple to make and guaranteed to become a mid-day favourite.*

INGREDIENTS

*Serves 4*

1 large cob sweetcorn

75 g/3 oz/¾ cup plain flour

1 egg

a little milk

2 large firm tomatoes

1 garlic clove, crushed

5 ml/1 tsp dried oregano

30–45 ml/2–3 tbsp olive oil, plus extra for
   shallow-frying

salt and freshly ground black pepper

8 cupped leaves iceberg lettuce, to serve

shredded fresh basil leaves, to garnish

1 Pull the husks and silk away from the corn, then hold the cob upright on a board and cut downwards with a heavy knife to strip off the kernels. Put the kernels in a pan of boiling water and cook for 3 minutes after the water has returned to the boil, then drain and rinse under the cold tap to cool quickly.

2 Put the flour into a bowl and break the egg into a well in the middle. Start stirring with a fork, adding a little milk to make a soft dropping consistency. Stir in the drained corn and season with salt and pepper.

3 Preheat the grill. Halve the tomatoes horizontally and make two or three criss-cross slashes across the cut side of each half. Rub in the crushed garlic and the oregano and season with salt and pepper. Trickle with oil and grill until lightly browned.

4 While the tomatoes grill, heat some oil in a wide frying pan and drop a tablespoon of batter into the centre. Cook, one at a time, over a low heat and turn as soon as the top is set. Drain on kitchen paper and keep warm while cooking the remaining fritters. The mixture should make at least 8 sweetcorn cakes.

5 For each serving, put 2 sweetcorn cakes on to lettuce leaves, garnish with basil and serve with a grilled tomato half.

# Cheese-stuffed Pears

*These pears, with their scrumptious creamy topping, make a sublime dish when served with a simple salad.*

INGREDIENTS

*Serves 4*

50 g/2 oz/¼ cup ricotta cheese

50 g/2 oz/¼ cup dolcelatte cheese

15 ml/1 tbsp honey

½ celery stick, finely sliced

8 green olives, pitted and roughly
  chopped

4 dates, stoned and cut into thin strips

pinch of paprika

4 ripe pears

150 ml/¼ pint/⅔ cup apple juice

1 Preheat the oven to 200°C/400°F/Gas 6. Place the ricotta in a bowl and crumble in the dolcelatte. Add the rest of the ingredients except for the pears and apple juice and mix well.

2 Halve the pears lengthways and use a melon baller to remove the cores. Place in an ovenproof dish and divide the filling equally between them.

3 Pour in the apple juice and cover the dish with foil. Bake for 20 minutes or until the pears are tender.

4 Remove the foil and place the dish under a hot grill for 3 minutes. Serve immediately.

COOK'S TIP

Choose ripe pears in season such as Conference, William or Comice.

# Ratatouille

*A classic vegetable stew, packed full of fresh vegetables and herbs and absolutely bursting with wonderful flavour.*

INGREDIENTS

*Serves 4*

2 large aubergines, roughly chopped

4 courgettes, roughly chopped

150 ml/¼ pint/⅔ cup olive oil

2 onions, sliced

2 garlic cloves, chopped

1 large red pepper, seeded and roughly chopped

2 large yellow peppers, seeded and roughly chopped

sprig of fresh rosemary

sprig of fresh thyme

5 ml/1 tsp coriander seeds, crushed

3 plum tomatoes, skinned, seeded and chopped

8 basil leaves, torn

salt and freshly ground black pepper

sprigs of fresh parsley or basil, to garnish

1 Sprinkle the aubergines and courgettes with salt, then put them in a colander with a plate and a weight on top to extract the bitter juices. Leave for about 30 minutes.

2 Heat the olive oil in a large saucepan. Add the onions and fry gently for 6–7 minutes, until just softened. Add the garlic and cook for another 2 minutes.

3 Rinse the aubergines and courgettes and pat dry with a clean dish towel. Add to the pan with the peppers, increase the heat and sauté until the peppers are just turning brown.

4 Add the herbs and coriander seeds, then cover the pan and cook gently for about 40 minutes.

5 Add the tomatoes and season with salt and pepper. Cook gently for a further 10 minutes, until the vegetables are soft but not too mushy. Remove the sprigs of herbs. Stir in the torn basil leaves and check the seasoning. Leave to cool slightly and serve warm or cold, garnished with sprigs of parsley or basil.

# Mushroom Croustades

*The rich mushroom flavour of this filling is heightened by the addition of mushroom ketchup.*

INGREDIENTS

*Serves 2–4*

1 short French stick, about 25 cm/10 in

10 ml/2 tsp olive oil

250 g/9 oz open cup mushrooms, quartered

10 ml/2 tsp mushroom ketchup

10 ml/2.tsp lemon juice

30 ml/2 tbsp skimmed milk

30 ml/2 tbsp snipped fresh chives

salt and freshly ground black pepper

snipped fresh chives, to garnish

3 Place the mushrooms in a small saucepan with the mushroom ketchup, lemon juice and milk. Simmer for about 5 minutes, or until most of the liquid is evaporated.

4 Remove from the heat, then add the chives and season with salt and pepper. Spoon into the bread croustades and serve hot, garnished with snipped chives.

1 Preheat the oven to 200°C/400°F/Gas 6. Cut the French bread in half lengthways. Cut a scoop out of the soft middle of each half, leaving a thick border all the way round.

2 Brush the bread with oil, place on a baking sheet and bake for about 6–8 minutes, until golden and crisp.

# Sliced Frittata with Tomato Sauce

*This dish – cold frittata with a tomato sauce – is ideal for a light summer lunch.*

INGREDIENTS

*Serves 3–4*

6 eggs

30 ml/2 tbsp finely chopped fresh mixed herbs, such as basil, parsley, thyme and tarragon

40 g/1½ oz/¼ cup freshly grated Parmesan cheese

45 ml/3 tbsp olive oil

salt and freshly ground black pepper

*For the tomato sauce*

30 ml/2 tbsp olive oil

1 small onion, finely chopped

350 g/12 oz fresh tomatoes, chopped, or 400 g/14 oz can chopped tomatoes

1 garlic clove, chopped

salt and freshly ground black pepper

1 To make the frittata, break the eggs into a bowl and beat them lightly with a fork. Beat in the herbs and Parmesan. Season with salt and pepper. Heat the oil in a large non-stick or heavy frying pan until hot but not smoking.

2 Pour in the seasoned egg mixture. Cook, without stirring, until the frittata is puffed and golden brown underneath.

3 Take a large plate, place it upside down over the pan and, holding it firmly with oven gloves, turn the pan and the frittata over on to it. Slide the frittata back into the pan and continue cooking for about 3–4 minutes more until it is golden brown on the second side. Remove from the heat and allow to cool completely.

4 To make the tomato sauce, heat the oil in a medium-heavy saucepan. Add the onion and cook slowly until it is soft. Add the tomatoes, garlic and 60 ml/ 4 tbsp water and season with salt and pepper. Cover the pan and cook over moderate heat for about 15 minutes.

5 Remove from the heat and cool slightly before pressing the sauce through a food mill or sieve. Leave to cool completely.

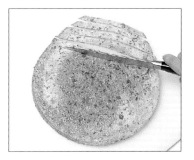

6 To assemble the salad, cut the frittata into thin slices. Place them in a serving bowl and toss lightly with the sauce. Serve at room temperature or chilled.

# Tomato Pesto Toasties

The flavour of pesto is so powerful
that it can be used in very small
amounts to good effect, as in these
tasty snacks.

## INGREDIENTS

*Serves 2*

2 thick slices crusty bread

45 ml/3 tbsp cream cheese or fromage
   frais

10 ml/2 tsp red or green pesto

1 beef tomato

1 red onion

salt and freshly ground black pepper

chopped basil, to garnish

1 Toast the bread slices until
golden brown on both sides.
Leave to cool.

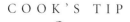

2 Mix together the cheese and
pesto in a small bowl until well
blended, then spread thickly on the
toasted bread.

3 Using a large sharp knife, cut
the beef tomato and red onion
crossways into thin slices.

4 Arrange the tomato and onion
slices, overlapping, on the toast
and season with salt and pepper.
Transfer to a grill rack and heat
through under a hot grill. Serve,
garnished with chopped basil.

## COOK'S TIP

Almost any type of crusty bread
can be used for this recipe, but
Italian olive oil bread and French
bread will give the best flavour.

# Gado Gado

*The peanut sauce on this traditional Indonesian vegetable dish owes its flavour to galangal, an aromatic rhizome that resembles ginger.*

INGREDIENTS

*Serves 4*

250 g/9 oz white cabbage, shredded

4 carrots, cut into matchsticks

4 celery sticks, cut into matchsticks

250 g/9 oz/4 cups beansprouts

½ cucumber, cut into matchsticks

fried onion, salted peanuts and sliced
    fresh chilli, to garnish

*For the peanut sauce*

15 ml/1 tbsp oil

1 small onion, finely chopped

1 garlic clove, crushed

1 small piece galangal, peeled and grated

5 ml/1 tsp ground cumin

1.5 ml/¼ tsp ground chilli powder

5 ml/1 tsp tamarind paste or lime juice

60 ml/4 tbsp crunchy peanut butter

5 ml/1 tsp soft light brown sugar

1 Steam the cabbage, carrots and celery for about 3–4 minutes, until just tender. Leave to cool. Spread out the beansprouts on a large serving dish. Arrange the cabbage, carrots, celery and cucumber on top.

2 To make the sauce, heat the oil in a saucepan, add the onion and garlic and cook gently for 5 minutes, until soft.

## COOK'S TIP

As long as the sauce remains the same, the vegetables can be altered at the whim of the cook and to reflect the contents of the vegetable rack or chiller.

3 Stir in the spices and cook for 1 minute more. Add the tamarind paste or lime juice, peanut butter and sugar. Mix well.

4 Heat the sauce gently, stirring occasionally and adding a little hot water if necessary, to make the sauce runny enough to coat the vegetables when poured.

5 Spoon a little of the sauce over the vegetables and toss lightly together. Garnish with fried onions, peanuts and sliced chilli. Serve the rest of the sauce in a bowl separately.

# Asparagus with Eggs

*The addition of fried eggs and grated Parmesan turns asparagus into something special.*

*Serves 4*

450 g/1 lb fresh asparagus

65 g/2½ oz/5 tbsp butter

4 eggs

60 ml/4 tbsp grated fresh Parmesan cheese

salt and freshly ground black pepper

4 As soon as the asparagus is cooked, remove it from the water with two slotted spoons. Place it on a wire rack covered with a clean dish towel to drain. Divide the spears between warm individual serving plates. Place a fried egg on each and sprinkle with the grated Parmesan.

5 Melt the remaining butter in the frying pan. As soon as it is bubbling, but before it browns, pour it over the cheese and eggs on the asparagus. Season with salt and pepper and serve at once.

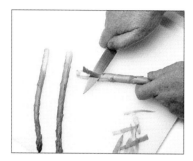

1 Cut off any woody ends from the asparagus. Peel the lower half of the spears by inserting a knife under the thick skin at the base and pulling up towards the tip. Wash the asparagus in cold water.

2 Bring a large pan of water to the boil. Boil the asparagus until just tender.

3 While the asparagus is cooking, melt a third of the butter in a frying pan. When bubbling, break in the eggs and cook them until the whites have set but the yolks are still soft.

# Cheese and Spinach Flan

*This flan freezes well and can be reheated. It makes an excellent addition to a festive buffet party.*

*Serves 8*

115 g/4 oz/8 tbsp butter

225 g/8 oz/2 cups plain flour

2.5 ml/½ tsp English mustard powder

2.5 ml/½ tsp paprika

large pinch of salt

115 g/4 oz Cheddar cheese, finely grated

1 egg, beaten, to glaze

*For the filling*

450 g/1 lb frozen spinach

1 onion, chopped

pinch of grated nutmeg

225 g/8 oz/1 cup cottage cheese

2 large eggs, beaten

50 g/2 oz freshly grated Parmesan cheese

150 ml/¼ pint/⅔ cup single cream

salt and freshly ground black pepper

1 Rub the butter into the flour until it resembles fine bread-crumbs. Stir in the mustard powder, paprika, salt and cheese. Bind to a dough with 45–60 ml/3–4 tbsp cold water. Knead until smooth, wrap and chill in the fridge for 30 minutes.

2 Put the spinach and onion in a pan, cover and cook slowly. Season with salt, pepper and nutmeg. Turn the spinach into a bowl and cool slightly. Add the remaining filling ingredients.

3 Roll out two-thirds of the pastry on a lightly floured surface and use it to line a 23 cm/9 in loose-based flan tin. Press it well into the edges, removing excess pastry with a rolling pin. Spoon the filling into the flan case.

4 Preheat the oven to 200°C/400°F/Gas 6. Put a baking tray in the oven to preheat.

5 Roll out the remaining pastry and cut it with a lattice pastry cutter. With the help of a rolling pin, lay it over the flan. Brush the joins with egg glaze. Press the edges together and trim off the excess pastry. Brush the pastry lattice with egg glaze and bake on the hot baking tray for 35–40 minutes, or until golden brown. Serve hot or cold.

# Curried Eggs

*Hard-boiled eggs are served on a bed of mild, creamy sauce with a hint of curry.*

INGREDIENTS

*Serves 2*

4 eggs

15 ml/1 tbsp sunflower oil

1 small onion, finely chopped

2.5 cm/1 in piece of fresh root ginger,
    peeled and grated

2.5 ml/½ tsp ground cumin

2.5 ml/½ tsp garam masala

7.5 ml/1½ tsp tomato paste

10 ml/2 tsp tandoori paste

10 ml/2 tsp lemon juice

250 ml/8 fl oz/¼ cup single cream

15 ml/1 tbsp chopped fresh coriander

salt and freshly ground black pepper

coriander sprigs, to garnish

1 Put the eggs in a pan of water. Bring to the boil, lower the heat and simmer for 10 minutes.

2 Meanwhile, heat the oil in a frying pan. Cook the onion for 2–3 minutes. Add the ginger and cook for 1 minute more.

3 Stir in the ground cumin, garam masala, tomato paste, tandoori paste, lemon juice and cream. Cook for 1–2 minutes, then stir in the coriander. Season with salt and pepper.

4 Drain the eggs, remove the shells and cut each egg in half. Spoon the sauce into a serving bowl, top with the eggs and garnish with coriander sprigs. Serve at once.

# Sweetcorn and Cheese Pasties

*These tasty pasties are really simple
to make and extremely moreish.
Why not make double – they'll go
like hot cakes.*

INGREDIENTS

*Makes 18–20*

250 g/9 oz sweetcorn

115 g/4 oz feta cheese

1 egg, beaten

30 ml/2 tbsp whipping cream

15 g/½ oz freshly grated Parmesan cheese

3 spring onions, chopped

8-10 small sheets filo pastry

115 g/4 oz/8 tbsp butter, melted

freshly ground black pepper

1 Preheat the oven to
190°C/375°F/Gas 5. Butter two
bun tins.

2 If using fresh sweetcorn, strip
the kernels from the cob using
a large sharp knife, cutting
downwards from top to bottom of
the cob. Simmer in a little salted
water for 3–5 minutes, until
tender. For canned sweetcorn,
drain and rinse well under cold
running water.

3 Crumble the feta cheese into a
bowl and stir in the sweetcorn.
Add the egg, cream, Parmesan
cheese, spring onions and ground
black pepper and stir well.

4 Take one sheet of pastry and
cut it in half to make a square.
(Keep the remaining pastry
covered with a damp cloth to
prevent it from drying out.) Brush
with melted butter and then fold
into four to make a smaller square
(about 7.5 cm/3 in).

5 Place a heaped teaspoon of
mixture in the centre of each
pastry square and then squeeze the
pastry around the filling to make a
'money bag' casing.

6 Continue making pasties until
all the filling is used up. Brush
the outside of each 'bag' with any
remaining butter and then bake for
about 15 minutes, until golden
brown. Serve hot.

# Roquefort Tartlets

*These can be made in shallow bun tins to serve hot as a first course. You could also make them in tiny cocktail tins, to serve warm as appetizing bite-size snacks with a drink before a meal.*

*Makes 12*

175 g/6 oz/1½ cups plain flour

large pinch of salt

115 g/4 oz/8 tbsp butter

1 egg yolk

30 ml/2 tbsp cold water

*For the filling*

15 g/½ oz/1 tbsp butter

15 g/½ oz/2 tbsp flour

150 ml/¼ pint/⅔ cup milk

115 g/4 oz Roquefort cheese, crumbled

150 ml/¼ pint/⅔ cup double cream

2.5 ml/½ tsp dried mixed herbs

3 egg yolks

salt and freshly ground black pepper

1 To make the pastry, sift the flour and salt into a bowl and rub the butter into the flour until it resembles breadcrumbs. Mix the egg yolk with the water and stir into the flour to make a soft dough. Knead until smooth, wrap in clear film and chill for 30 minutes. (You can also make the dough in a food processor.)

2 In a saucepan, melt the butter, stir in the flour and then the milk. Boil to thicken, stirring continuously. Off the heat, beat in the cheese and season with salt and pepper. Cool. In another saucepan, bring the cream and herbs to the boil and cook until the liquid has reduced to 30 ml/2 tbsp. Beat into the cheese sauce with the eggs.

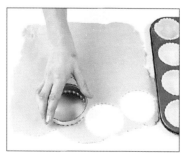

3 Preheat the oven to 190°C/375°F/Gas 5. On a lightly floured work surface, roll out the pastry to 3 mm/⅛ in thick. Stamp out rounds with a fluted cutter and use to line your chosen bun tins.

4 Divide the filling between the tartlets; they should be filled or two-thirds full. Stamp out smaller fluted rounds or star shapes for the tops and lay on top of each tartlet. Bake for 20–25 minutes, or until golden brown.

# Stuffed Mushrooms

*This is a classic mushroom dish, strongly flavoured with garlic. Use flat mushrooms or field mushrooms that are sometimes available from farm shops.*

*Serves 4*

450 g/1 lb large flat mushrooms

butter, for greasing

about 75 ml/5 tbsp olive oil

2 garlic cloves, crushed

45 ml/3 tbsp finely chopped fresh parsley

40–50 g/1½–2 oz/¾–1 cup fresh white breadcrumbs

salt and freshly ground black pepper

sprig of fresh flat leaf parsley, to garnish

1 Preheat the oven to 180°C/350°F/Gas 4. Cut off the mushroom stalks and reserve.

2 Arrange the mushroom caps in a buttered shallow dish, gill side upwards.

3 Heat 15 ml/1 tbsp of the oil in a frying pan and fry the garlic briefly. Finely chop the mushroom stalks and mix with the parsley and breadcrumbs. Add the garlic and 15 ml/1 tbsp of the oil. Season with salt and pepper. Pile a little of the mixture into each mushroom.

4 Add the remaining oil to the dish and cover the mushrooms with buttered greaseproof paper. Bake for 15–20 minutes, removing the paper for the last five minutes to brown the tops. Garnish with a sprig of flat leaf parsley.

# SALADS

# Spicy Bean and Lentil Loaf

*An appetizing, high-fibre savoury loaf, ideal for packed lunches.*

INGREDIENTS

*Serves 12*

10 ml/2 tsp olive oil

1 onion, finely chopped

1 garlic clove, crushed

2 celery sticks, finely chopped

400 g/14 oz can red kidney beans

400 g/14 oz can lentils

1 egg

1 carrot, coarsely grated

50 g/2 oz/½ cup finely grated mature
    Cheddar cheese

50 g/2 oz/1 cup fresh wholemeal
    breadcrumbs

15 ml/1 tbsp tomato purée

15 ml/1 tbsp tomato ketchup

5 ml/1 tsp each ground cumin, ground
    coriander and hot chilli powder

salt and freshly ground black pepper

salad, to serve

1 Preheat the oven to 180°C/350°F/Gas 4. Lightly grease a 900 g/2 lb loaf tin.

2 Heat the oil in a saucepan, add the onion, garlic and celery and cook gently for 5 minutes, stirring occasionally. Remove the pan from the heat and cool slightly.

3 Rinse and drain the beans and lentils. Put in a blender or food processor with the onion mixture and egg and process until smooth.

4 Transfer the mixture to a bowl, add all the remaining ingredients and mix well. Season with salt and pepper.

5 Spoon the mixture into the prepared tin and level the surface. Bake for about 1 hour, then remove from the tin and serve hot or cold in slices, accompanied by a salad.

# Pear and Pecan Salad with Blue Cheese

*Toasted pecan nuts have a special union with crisp white pears. Their robust flavours combine especially well with a rich blue cheese dressing and make this a salad to remember.*

INGREDIENTS

*Serves 4*

75 g/3 oz/½ cup shelled pecan nuts, roughly chopped

3 crisp pears

175 g/6 oz young spinach, stems removed

1 escarole or butterhead lettuce

1 radicchio

30 ml/2 tbsp ready-made blue cheese dressing

salt and freshly ground black pepper

crusty bread, to serve

1 Toast the pecan nuts under a moderate grill, to bring out their flavour.

2 Cut the pears into even slices, leaving the skin intact and discarding the cores.

3 Wash the salad leaves and spin dry. Add the pears together with the toasted pecans, then toss with the dressing. Distribute between 4 large plates and season with salt and pepper. Serve with warm crusty bread.

## VARIATION

If you want a lighter non-cheese dressing, combine 5 ml/1 tsp of wholegrain mustard, 2.5 ml/½ tsp of granulated sugar, 1.5 ml/¼ tsp of dried tarragon, 10 ml/2 tsp of lemon juice and 60 ml/4 tbsp of olive oil in a jar and shake vigorously.

# Savoury Nut Loaf

*This delicious nut loaf makes perfect picnic food.*

*Serves 4*

15 ml/1 tbsp olive oil, plus extra for
   greasing
1 onion, chopped
1 leek, chopped
2 celery sticks, finely chopped
225 g/8 oz mushrooms, chopped
2 garlic cloves, crushed
425 g/15 oz can lentils, rinsed and drained
115 g/4 oz/1 cup mixed nuts, such as
   hazelnuts, cashew nuts and almonds,
   finely chopped
50 g/2 oz/½ cup flour
50 g/2 oz/½ cup grated mature Cheddar
   cheese
1 medium egg, beaten
45–60 ml/3–4 tbsp chopped fresh
   mixed herbs
salt and freshly ground black pepper
chives and sprigs of fresh flat leaf parsley,
   to garnish

1 Preheat the oven to
190°C/375°F/Gas 5. Lightly
grease the base and sides of a
900 g/2 lb loaf tin and line with
greaseproof paper.

2 Heat the oil in a large
saucepan, add the chopped
onion, leek, celery sticks and
mushrooms and the crushed
garlic, then cook gently for 10
minutes, until the vegetables have
softened, stirring occasionally.

3 Add the lentils, mixed nuts,
flour, grated cheese, egg and
herbs. Season with salt and pepper
and mix thoroughly.

4 Spoon the nut, vegetable and
lentil mixture into the
prepared loaf tin, ensuring that it
is pressed into the corners, and
level the surface. Bake, uncovered,
for 50–60 minutes, or until the nut
loaf is lightly browned on top and
firm to the touch.

5 Cool the loaf slightly in the
tin, then turn out on to a
serving plate. Serve hot or cold, cut
into slices and garnished with
chives and flat leaf parsley.

# New Spring Vegetable Salad

*This chunky salad makes a satisfying meal. Use other spring vegetables, if you like.*

*Serves 4*

675 g/1½ lb small new potatoes, halved

400 g/14 oz can broad beans, drained

115 g/4 oz cherry tomatoes

75 g/3 oz/½ cup walnut halves

30 ml/2 tbsp white wine vinegar

15 ml/1 tbsp wholegrain mustard

60 ml/4 tbsp olive oil

pinch of sugar

225 g/8 oz young asparagus
    spears, trimmed

6 spring onions, trimmed

salt and freshly ground black pepper

baby spinach leaves, to serve

1 Put the potatoes in a saucepan. Cover with cold water and bring to the boil. Cook for 10–12 minutes, until tender. Meanwhile, put the broad beans in a bowl. Cut the tomatoes in half and add them to the bowl with the walnuts.

2 Put the white wine vinegar, mustard, olive oil and sugar into a jar. Season with salt and pepper. Close the jar tightly and shake well.

3 Add the asparagus to the potatoes and cook for 3 minutes more. Drain the cooked vegetables well. Cool under cold running water and drain again. Thickly slice the potatoes and cut the spring onions in half.

4 Add the asparagus, potatoes and spring onions to the bowl containing the broad bean mixture. Pour the dressing over the salad and toss well. Serve on a bed of baby spinach leaves.

# Chinese Garlic Mushrooms

*Tofu is high in protein and very low in fat, so it is a very useful food to keep handy for quick meals and snacks like this one.*

INGREDIENTS

*Serves 4*

8 large open-cap mushrooms

3 spring onions, sliced

1 garlic clove, crushed

30 ml/2 tbsp mushroom sauce

275 g/10 oz packet marinated tofu
(beancurd), cut into small dice

200 g/7 oz can sweetcorn, drained

10 ml/2 tsp sesame oil

salt and freshly ground black pepper

1 Preheat the oven to 200°C/400°F/Gas 6. Finely chop the mushroom stalks and mix with the spring onions, garlic and mushroom sauce.

2 Stir in the diced marinated tofu and sweetcorn, season with salt and pepper, then spoon the filling into the mushrooms.

3 Brush the edges of the mushrooms with the sesame oil. Arrange the stuffed mushrooms in a baking dish and bake for 12–15 minutes, until the mushrooms are just tender, then serve at once.

COOK'S TIP

If you prefer, omit the mushroom sauce and use light soy sauce instead.

# Couscous Salad

*This is a spicy variation on a classic lemon-flavoured tabbouleh, which is traditionally made with bulgur wheat, rather than couscous.*

INGREDIENTS

*Serves 4*

45 ml/3 tbsp olive oil

5 spring onions, chopped

1 garlic clove, crushed

1 tsp ground cumin

350 ml/12 fl oz/1½ cups vegetable stock

175 g/6 oz/1 cup couscous

2 tomatoes, peeled and chopped

60 ml/4 tbsp chopped fresh parsley

60 ml/4 tbsp chopped fresh mint

1 fresh green chilli, seeded and
    finely chopped

30 ml/2 tbsp lemon juice

salt and freshly ground black pepper

toasted pine nuts and grated lemon rind,
    to garnish

crisp lettuce leaves, to serve

1 Heat the oil in a saucepan. Add the spring onions and garlic. Stir in the cumin and cook for 1 minute. Add the stock and bring to the boil.

2 Remove the pan from the heat, stir in the couscous, cover the pan and leave it to stand for 10 minutes, until the couscous has swelled and all the liquid has been absorbed. If you are using instant couscous, follow the package instructions.

3 Tip the couscous into a bowl. Stir in the tomatoes, parsley, mint, chilli and lemon juice. Season with salt and pepper. If possible, leave to stand for up to an hour, to allow the flavours to develop fully.

4 To serve, line a bowl with lettuce leaves and spoon the couscous salad over the top. Scatter the toasted pine nuts and grated lemon rind over the top, to garnish.

# Baked Eggs with Creamy Leeks

*This is a traditional French way of enjoying eggs. You can vary the dish quite easily by experimenting with other vegetables, such as puréed spinach or ratatouille, as a base.*

*Serves 4*

15 g/½ oz/1 tbsp butter, plus extra
    for greasing

225 g/8 oz small leeks, thinly sliced

75–90 ml/5–6 tbsp whipping cream

freshly grated nutmeg

4 eggs

salt and freshly ground black pepper

1 Preheat the oven to 190°C/375°F/Gas 5. Generously butter the base and sides of four ramekin dishes or individual soufflé dishes.

2 Melt the butter in a small frying pan and cook the leeks over medium heat, stirring frequently, until softened but not browned.

---

### VARIATION
~

Put 15 ml/1 tbsp of cream in each dish with some chopped herbs. Break in the eggs, add 15 ml/1 tbsp cream and a little grated cheese, then bake.

---

3 Add 45 ml/3 tbsp of the cream and cook gently for about 5 minutes, until the leeks are very soft and the cream has thickened a little. Season with salt, pepper and nutmeg.

4 Arrange the ramekins in a small roasting tin and divide the leeks among them. Break an egg into each, spoon 5–10 ml/ 1–2 tsp of the remaining cream over each egg and season lightly.

5 Pour boiling water into the roasting tin to come halfway up the side of the ramekins or soufflé dishes. Bake for about 10 minutes, until the whites are set and the yolks are still soft, or a little longer if you prefer them more well done.

# Brown Bean Salad

Brown beans, sometimes called 'ful medames', are widely used in Egyptian cooking, and are occasionally seen in health food shops here. Dried broad beans, black or kidney beans make a good substitute.

INGREDIENTS

Serves 6

350 g/12 oz/1½ cups dried brown beans

2 sprigs of fresh thyme

2 bay leaves

1 onion, halved

4 garlic cloves, crushed

2.5 ml/1½ tsp cumin seeds, crushed

3 spring onions, finely chopped

90 ml/6 tbsp chopped fresh parsley

20 ml/4 tsp lemon juice

90 ml/6 tbsp olive oil

3 hard-boiled eggs, shelled and
   roughly chopped

1 pickled cucumber, roughly chopped

salt and freshly ground black pepper

1 Put the beans in a bowl with plenty of cold water and leave to soak overnight. Drain, transfer to a saucepan and cover with fresh water. Bring to the boil and boil rapidly for 10 minutes.

COOK'S TIP

The cooking time for dried beans can vary considerably. They may need only 45 minutes, or a lot longer.

2 Reduce the heat and add the thyme, bay leaves and onion. Simmer very gently for about 1 hour, until tender. Drain and discard the herbs and onion.

3 Mix together the garlic, cumin, spring onions, parsley, lemon juice and oil. Season with salt and pepper. Pour over the beans and toss lightly together. Gently stir in the eggs and cucumber and serve at once.

# Vegetable Fajitas

*A colourful medley of mushrooms
and peppers in a spicy sauce,
wrapped in tortillas and served with
creamy guacamole.*

INGREDIENTS

*Serves 2*

1 onion

1 red pepper

1 green pepper

1 yellow pepper

1 garlic clove, crushed

225 g/8 oz mushrooms

90 ml/6 tbsp vegetable oil

30 ml/2 tbsp medium chilli powder

salt and freshly ground black pepper

*For the guacamole*

1 ripe avocado

1 shallot, coarsely chopped

1 fresh green chilli, seeded and
   coarsely chopped

juice of 1 lime

*To serve*

4–6 flour tortillas, warmed

1 lime, cut into wedges

sprigs of fresh coriander

1 Slice the onion. Cut the
peppers in half, remove the
seeds and cut the flesh into strips.
Combine the onion and peppers in
a bowl. Add the crushed garlic and
mix lightly.

2 Remove the mushroom stalks.
Save for making stock, or
discard. Slice the mushroom caps
and add to the pepper mixture in
the bowl. Mix the oil and chilli
powder in a cup, pour over the
vegetable mixture and stir well.
Set aside.

3 Make the guacamole. Cut the
avocado in half and remove
the stone and the peel. Put the
flesh into a food processor or
blender with the shallot, green
chilli and lime juice.

4 Process for 1 minute, until
smooth. Scrape into a small
bowl, cover tightly and put in the
fridge to chill until required.

5 Heat a frying pan or wok until
very hot. Add the marinated
vegetables and stir-fry over high
heat for 5–6 minutes, until the
mushrooms and peppers are just
tender. Season with salt and
pepper. Spoon the filling on to
each tortilla and roll up. Garnish
with coriander and serve with the
guacamole and lime wedges.

# Pepper and Wild Mushroom Pasta Salad

*A combination of grilled peppers and wild mushrooms makes this pasta salad colourful as well as nutritious.*

*Serves 6*

1 red pepper, halved

1 yellow pepper, halved

1 green pepper, halved

350 g/12 oz wholewheat pasta shells
   or twists

30 ml/2 tbsp olive oil

45 ml/3 tbsp balsamic vinegar

75 ml/5 tbsp tomato juice

30 ml/2 tbsp chopped fresh basil

15 ml/1 tbsp chopped fresh thyme

175 g/6 oz shiitake mushrooms, sliced

175 g/6 oz oyster mushrooms, sliced

400 g/14 oz can black-eyed beans, rinsed
   and drained

115 g/4 oz/²⁄₃ cup sultanas

2 bunches spring onions, finely chopped

salt and freshly ground black pepper

2 Meanwhile, cook the pasta in lightly salted boiling water for 10–12 minutes, until tender, then drain thoroughly.

3 Mix together the oil, vinegar, tomato juice, fresh basil and thyme. Add to the warm pasta and toss together.

4 Remove and discard the skins from the peppers. Seed and slice the peppers and add to the pasta with the mushrooms, beans, sultanas and spring onions. Season with salt and pepper. Toss the ingredients to mix and serve immediately or cover and chill in the fridge before serving.

1 Preheat the grill. Put the peppers cut-side down on a grill pan rack and place under the hot grill for 10–15 minutes, until the skins are charred. Cover the peppers with a clean, damp dish towel and set aside to cool.

# Frittata with Sun-dried Tomatoes

*Adding just a few sun-dried
tomatoes gives this frittata a
distinctly Mediterranean flavour.*

### INGREDIENTS

*Serves 3–4*

6 sun-dried tomatoes, dry or in oil and
    drained

60 ml/4 tbsp olive oil

1 small onion, finely chopped

pinch of fresh thyme leaves

6 eggs

50 g/2 oz/½ cup freshly grated Parmesan
    cheese

salt and freshly ground black pepper

1 Place the tomatoes in a small
bowl and pour on enough hot
water to just cover them. Soak for
about 15 minutes. Lift the
tomatoes out of the water and slice
them into thin strips. Reserve the
soaking water.

2 Heat the oil in a large non-
stick or heavy frying pan. Stir
in the onion and cook for 5–6
minutes or until soft and golden.
Add the tomatoes and thyme and
continue to stir over moderate
heat for 2–3 minutes. Season with
salt and pepper.

3 Break the eggs into a bowl and
beat lightly with a fork. Stir in
45–60 ml/3–4 tbsp of the tomato
soaking water and the grated
Parmesan cheese.

4 Raise the heat under the pan.
When the oil is sizzling, pour
in the eggs. Mix them quickly into
the other ingredients and stop
stirring. Lower the heat to
moderate and cook for 4–5
minutes on the first side, or until
the frittata is puffed and golden
brown underneath.

5 Take a large plate, place it
upside down over the pan and,
holding it firmly with oven gloves,
turn the pan and the frittata over
on to it. Slide the frittata back into
the pan and continue cooking
until golden brown on the second
side, 3–4 minutes more. Remove
from the heat. The frittata can be
served hot, at room temperature or
cold. Cut it into wedges to serve.

# Wholewheat Pasta Salad

*This substantial salad is easily assembled from any combination of seasonal vegetables.*

INGREDIENTS

*Serves 8*

450 g/1 lb short wholewheat pasta, such as
   fusilli or penne

45 ml/3 tbsp olive oil

2 medium carrots

1 small head broccoli

175 g/6 oz/1 cup shelled peas, fresh
   or frozen

1 red or yellow pepper, seeded

2 sticks celery

4 spring onions

1 large tomato

75 g/3 oz/½ cup stoned olives

*For the dressing*

45 ml/3 tbsp wine or balsamic vinegar

60 ml/4 tbsp olive oil

15 ml/1 tbsp Dijon mustard

15 ml/1 tbsp sesame seeds

10 ml/2 tsp chopped mixed fresh herbs
   such as parsley, thyme and basil

115 g/4 oz/⅔ cup diced Cheddar or
   mozzarella, or a combination of both

salt and freshly ground black pepper

coriander, to garnish

1 Cook the pasta in a large pan of rapidly boiling salted water until it is tender. Drain and rinse under cold water to stop the cooking.

2 Drain well and turn into a large bowl. Toss with 45 ml/ 3 tbsp of the olive oil and set aside. Allow to cool completely before mixing with the other ingredients.

3 Lightly blanch the carrots, broccoli and peas in a large pan of boiling water. Refresh under cold water. Drain well.

4 Chop the carrots and broccoli into bite-size pieces and add to the pasta with the peas. Slice the pepper, celery, spring onions and tomato into small pieces. Add them to the salad with the olives.

5 Make the dressing in a small bowl by combining the vinegar with the oil and mustard. Stir in the sesame seeds and herbs. Mix the dressing into the salad. Taste for seasoning, add salt and pepper or more oil and vinegar as necessary. Stir in the cheese. Allow the salad to stand for 15 minutes before serving. Garnish with coriander.

# Rice Noodles with Vegetable Chilli Sauce

*Fresh chilli and coriander combine to give this recipe quite a strong flavour kick.*

## INGREDIENTS

*Serves 4*

15 ml/1 tbsp sunflower oil

1 onion, chopped

2 garlic cloves, crushed

1 fresh red chilli, seeded and
    finely chopped

1 red pepper, seeded and diced

2 carrots, finely chopped

175 g/6 oz baby sweetcorn, halved

225 g/8 oz can sliced bamboo shoots,
    rinsed and drained

400 g/14 oz can red kidney beans, rinsed
    and drained

300 ml/½ pint/1¼ cups passata

15 ml/1 tbsp soy sauce

5 ml/1 tsp ground coriander

250 g/9 oz rice noodles

30 ml/2 tbsp chopped fresh coriander

salt and freshly ground black pepper

fresh parsley sprigs, to garnish

3 Meanwhile, place the noodles in a bowl and cover with boiling water. Stir with a fork and leave to stand for 3–4 minutes or according to the package instructions. Rinse and drain.

4 Stir the fresh coriander into the sauce. Spoon the noodles on to warmed serving plates, top with the sauce, garnish with parsley and serve.

1 Heat the oil in a saucepan, add the onion, garlic, chilli and red pepper and cook gently for 5 minutes, stirring. Add the carrots, sweetcorn, bamboo shoots, kidney beans, passata, soy sauce and ground coriander and stir to mix.

2 Bring to the boil, then cover and simmer gently for 30 minutes, stirring occasionally, until the vegetables are tender. Season with salt and pepper.

# Fruity Rice Salad

*An appetizing and colourful rice salad combining many different flavours, ideal for a packed lunch.*

INGREDIENTS

*Serves 4–6*

225 g/8 oz/1 cup mixed brown and
   wild rice
1 yellow pepper, seeded and diced
1 bunch spring onions, chopped
3 sticks celery, chopped
1 large beefsteak tomato, chopped
2 green-skinned eating apples, chopped
175 g/6 oz/¾ cup ready-to-eat dried
   apricots, chopped
115 g/4 oz/⅔ cup raisins
30 ml/2 tbsp unsweetened apple juice
30 ml/2 tbsp dry sherry
30 ml/2 tbsp light soy sauce
dash of Tabasco sauce
30 ml/2 tbsp chopped fresh parsley
15 ml/1 tbsp chopped fresh rosemary
salt and freshly ground black pepper

2 Place the pepper, spring onions, celery, tomato, apples, apricots, raisins and the cooked rice in a serving bowl and mix well.

3 In a small bowl, mix together the apple juice, sherry, soy sauce, Tabasco sauce and herbs. Season with salt and pepper.

4 Pour the dressing over the rice mixture and toss the ingredients together to mix. Serve immediately or cover and chill in the fridge before serving.

1 Cook the rice in a large saucepan of lightly salted boiling water for about 30 minutes (or according to the package instructions) until tender. Rinse the cooked rice under cold running water to cool quickly, and drain thoroughly.

# Stir-fried Vegetables with Cashew Nuts

*Stir-frying is the perfect way to make a delicious, colourful and very speedy meal.*

### INGREDIENTS

*Serves 4*

900 g/2 lb mixed vegetables (see Cook's Tip)

30–60 ml/2–4 tbsp sunflower or olive oil

2 garlic cloves, crushed

15 ml/1 tbsp grated fresh root ginger

50 g/2 oz/½ cup cashew nuts or 60 ml/ 4 tbsp sunflower seeds, pumpkin seeds or sesame seeds

soy sauce

salt and freshly ground black pepper

1 Prepare the vegetables according to type. Carrots and cucumber should be cut into very fine matchsticks.

## COOK'S TIP
~

Use a pack of stir-fry vegetables or make up your own mixture. Choose from carrots, mangetouts, baby sweetcorn, pak choi, cucumber, beansprouts, mushrooms, peppers and spring onions. Drained canned bamboo shoots and water chestnuts are delicious additions.

2 Heat a frying pan, then trickle the oil around the rim so that it runs down to coat the surface. When the oil is hot, add the garlic and ginger and cook for 2–3 minutes, stirring. Add the harder vegetables and toss over the heat for a further 5 minutes, until they start to soften.

3 Add the softer vegetables and stir-fry all of them over a high heat for 3–4 minutes.

4 Stir in the cashew nuts or seeds. Season with soy sauce, salt and pepper. Serve at once.

# Marinated Cucumber Salad

*Sprinkling the cucumber with salt draws out some of the water and makes them crisper.*

INGREDIENTS

*Serves 4–6*

2 medium cucumbers

15 ml/1 tbsp salt

90 g/3½ oz/½ cup granulated sugar

175 ml/6 fl oz/¾ cup dry cider

15 ml/1 tbsp cider vinegar

45 ml/3 tbsp chopped fresh dill

pinch of freshly ground black pepper

sprig of dill, to garnish

1 Slice the cucumbers thinly and place them in a colander, sprinkling salt between each layer. Put the colander over a bowl and leave to drain for 1 hour.

2 Thoroughly rinse the cucumber slices under cold running water to remove excess salt, then pat dry on absorbent kitchen paper.

3 Gently heat the sugar, cider and vinegar in a saucepan, until the sugar has dissolved. Remove from the heat and leave to cool. Put the cucumber slices in a bowl, pour over the cider mixture and leave to marinate for 2 hours.

4 Drain the cucumber and sprinkle with the dill and pepper to taste. Mix well and transfer to a serving dish. Garnish with a sprig of dill. Chill in the fridge until ready to serve.

# Peanut Noodles

*Add any of your favourite vegetables to this quick lunch recipe – and increase the quantity of chilli, if you can take the heat!*

INGREDIENTS

*Serves 4*

200 g/7 oz medium egg noodles

30 ml/2 tbsp olive oil

2 garlic cloves, crushed

1 large onion, roughly chopped

1 red pepper, seeded and roughly chopped

1 yellow pepper, seeded and roughly chopped

350 g/12 oz courgettes, roughly chopped

150 g/5 oz/generous ¾ cup roasted unsalted peanuts, roughly chopped

*For the dressing*

50 ml/2 fl oz/¼ cup olive oil

grated rind and juice of 1 lemon

1 fresh red chilli, seeded and finely chopped

45 ml/3 tbsp snipped fresh chives

15–30 ml/1–2 tbsp balsamic vinegar

salt and freshly ground black pepper

snipped fresh chives, to garnish

1 Cook the noodles according to the package instructions and drain well.

2 Meanwhile, heat the oil in a very large frying pan or wok and cook the garlic and onion for 3 minutes, or until beginning to soften. Add the peppers and cour-gettes and cook for a further 15 minutes over a medium heat until beginning to soften and brown. Add the peanuts and cook for a further 1 minute.

3 Whisk together the olive oil, grated lemon rind and 45 ml/ 3 tbsp of the lemon juice, the chilli, chives and balsamic vinegar to taste. Season with salt and pepper.

4 Toss the noodles into the vegetables and stir-fry to heat through. Add the dressing, stir to coat and serve immediately, garnished with fresh chives.

# Classic Greek Salad

*If you have ever visited Greece, you'll know that a Greek salad with a chunk of bread makes a delicious, filling meal.*

INGREDIENTS

*Serves 4*

1 romaine lettuce

½ cucumber, halved lengthwise

4 tomatoes

8 spring onions

50 g/2 oz/⅓ cup Greek black olives

115 g/4 oz feta cheese

90 ml/6 tbsp white wine vinegar

120 ml/4 fl oz/½ cup olive oil

salt and freshly ground black pepper

olives and bread, to serve (optional)

3 Slice the spring onions. Add them to the bowl with the olives and toss well.

4 Cut the feta cheese into cubes and add to the salad.

5 Put the vinegar, olive oil and salt and pepper into a small bowl and whisk well. Pour the dressing over the salad and toss to combine. Serve at once, with olives and chunks of bread, if desired.

1 Tear the lettuce into pieces, and place them in a large mixing bowl. Slice the cucumber and add to the bowl.

2 Cut the tomatoes into wedges and put them into the bowl.

## COOK'S TIP

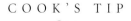

The salad can be assembled in advance and chilled, but add the lettuce and dressing just before serving. Keep the dressing at room temperature, as chilling deadens its flavour.

# Penne with Fennel, Tomato and Blue Cheese

*The anise flavour of the fennel makes it the perfect partner for tomato, especially when topped with blue cheese.*

### INGREDIENTS

*Serves 2*

1 fennel bulb

225 g/8 oz/2 cups penne or other dried
 pasta shapes

30 ml/2 tbsp olive oil

1 shallot, finely chopped

300 ml/½ pint/1¼ cups passata

pinch of sugar

5 ml/1 tsp chopped fresh oregano

115 g/4 oz blue cheese

salt and freshly ground black pepper

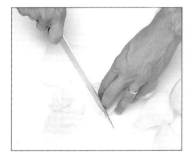

1 Cut the fennel bulb in half. Cut away the hard core and root. Slice the fennel thinly, then cut the slices into strips.

2 Bring a large pan of salted water to the boil. Add the pasta and cook for 10–12 minutes, until just tender.

3 Meanwhile, heat the oil in a small saucepan. Add the fennel and shallot and cook for 2–3 minutes over high heat, stirring occasionally.

4 Add the passata, sugar and oregano. Cover the pan and simmer gently for 10–12 minutes, until the fennel is tender. Season with salt and pepper. Drain the pasta and return it to the pan. Toss with the sauce. Serve with blue cheese crumbled over the top.

# Fresh Spinach and Avocado Salad

*Young, tender spinach leaves make a change from lettuce and are delicious served with avocado, cherry tomatoes and radishes in a tofu sauce.*

INGREDIENTS

*Serves 2–3*

1 large avocado

juice of 1 lime

225 g/8 oz fresh baby spinach leaves

115 g/4 oz cherry tomatoes

4 spring onions, sliced

½ cucumber

50 g/2 oz radishes, sliced

*For the dressing*

115 g/4 oz soft silken tofu

45 ml/3 tbsp milk

10 ml/2 tsp prepared mustard

2.5 ml/½ tsp white wine vinegar

pinch of cayenne, plus extra to serve

salt and freshly ground black pepper

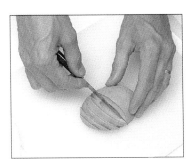

1 Cut the avocado in half, remove the stone, and strip off the skin. Cut the flesh into slices. Transfer to a plate, drizzle over the lime juice, and set aside.

### COOK'S TIP
~

Use soft, silken tofu rather than the firm block variety. It can be found in most supermarkets in long-life cartons.

2 Wash and dry the spinach leaves. Put them in a mixing bowl.

3 Cut the larger cherry tomatoes in half, and add all the tomatoes to the mixing bowl, with the spring onions. Cut the cucumber into chunks, and add to the bowl with the sliced radishes.

4 Make the dressing. Put the tofu, milk, mustard, wine vinegar and cayenne in a food processor or blender. Add salt and pepper to taste. Process for 30 seconds until smooth. Scrape the dressing into a bowl, and add a little extra milk if you like a thinner dressing. Sprinkle with a little extra cayenne, and garnish with radish roses and herb sprigs.

# Pasta with Pesto Sauce

*Don't stint on the fresh basil – this is the most wonderful sauce in the world! And it tastes completely different from the ready-made pesto sold in jars.*

*Serves 4*

2 garlic cloves

50g/2oz/½ cup pine nuts

40g/1½oz/1 cup fresh basil leaves

150ml/¼ pint/⅔ cup olive oil

50g/2oz/4 tbsp unsalted butter, softened

60ml/4 tbsp freshly grated
   Parmesan cheese

450g/1lb spaghetti

salt and ground black pepper

1 Peel the garlic and process in a blender or food processor with a little salt and the pine nuts until broken up. Add the basil leaves and continue mixing to a paste.

2 Gradually add the olive oil, little by little, until the mixture is creamy and thick.

3 Beat in the butter and season with ground black pepper. Beat in the cheese. Alternatively, you can make the pesto by hand using a pestle and mortar.

4 Store the pesto sauce in a jar, with a layer of olive oil on top to exclude the air, in the fridge until needed.

5 Cook the pasta in plenty of boiling salted water according to the instructions on the packet, until *al dente*. Drain well.

6 Toss the pasta with half the pesto and serve in warm bowls, with the remaining pesto sauce spooned over the top.

# Sweet and Sour Peppers with Pasta Bows

*A zesty dressing makes this simple pasta salad really special.*

INGREDIENTS

*Serves 4–6*

1 each red, yellow and orange pepper
1 garlic clove, crushed
30 ml/2 tbsp capers
30 ml/2 tbsp raisins
5 ml/1 tsp wholegrain mustard
grated rind and juice of 1 lime
5 ml/1 tsp runny honey
30 ml/2 tbsp chopped fresh coriander
225 g/8 oz pasta bows
salt and freshly ground black pepper
shavings of Parmesan cheese, to
    serve (optional)

1 Quarter the peppers and remove the stalks and seeds. Put into boiling water and cook for 10–15 minutes, until tender. Drain and rinse under cold water. Peel away the skins and seeds and cut the flesh lengthways into strips.

2 Put the garlic, capers, raisins, mustard, lime rind and juice, honey and coriander into a bowl. Season with salt and pepper and whisk together.

3 Cook the pasta in a large pan of boiling salted water for 10–12 minutes, until tender. Drain thoroughly.

4 Return the pasta to the pan, add the peppers and dressing. Heat gently and toss to mix. Transfer to a warm serving bowl. Serve with a few shavings of Parmesan cheese, if using.

# Pasta Primavera

*There's no better way to showcase
the best of the spring season's young
vegetables than in this delightful
pasta dish.*

INGREDIENTS

Serves 4

225 g/8 oz thin asparagus spears, cut in
  half
115 g/4 oz mangetouts, topped and tailed
115 g/4 oz whole baby sweetcorn
225 g/8 oz whole baby carrots
1 small red pepper, seeded and chopped
8 spring onions, sliced
225 g/8 oz torchietti
150 ml/¼ pint/⅔ cup cottage cheese
150 ml/¼ pint/⅔ cup low-fat yogurt
15 ml/1 tbsp lemon juice
15 ml/1 tbsp chopped fresh parsley
milk (optional)
15 ml/1 tbsp snipped chives
salt and freshly ground black pepper
sun-dried tomato bread, to serve

3 Cook the pasta in a large pan
of boiling salted water until
tender. Drain thoroughly. Put the
cottage cheese, yogurt, lemon juice
and parsley into a food processor
or blender. Season with salt and
pepper, then process until smooth.
Thin the sauce with a little milk,
if necessary.

4 Put the sauce into a large pan
with the pasta and vegetables,
heat gently and toss carefully.
Transfer to a warmed serving
plate, scatter the chives over the
top and serve with sun-dried
tomato bread.

1 Cook the thin asparagus spears
in a pan of boiling salted water
for 3–4 minutes. Add the
mangetouts halfway through the
cooking time. Drain and rinse
both under cold water.

2 Cook the baby sweetcorn,
carrots, red pepper and spring
onions in the same way until
tender. Drain and rinse.

# Bulgur Wheat and Broad Bean Salad

This appetizing salad is ideal served with fresh crusty wholemeal bread and home-made chutney or pickle.

## INGREDIENTS

Serves 6

350 g/12 oz/2 cups bulgur wheat
225 g/8 oz frozen broad beans
115 g/4 oz/1 cup frozen petit pois
225 g/8 oz cherry tomatoes, halved
1 Spanish onion, chopped
1 red pepper, seeded and chopped
50 g/2 oz mangetouts, chopped
50 g/2 oz watercress
15 ml/1 tbsp chopped fresh parsley
15 ml/1 tbsp chopped fresh basil
15 ml/1 tbsp chopped fresh thyme
French dressing
salt and freshly ground black pepper

3 Add the cherry tomatoes, onion, pepper, mangetouts and watercress to the bulgur wheat mixture. Toss well together in the bowl until all the ingredients are well-combined.

4 Add the chopped fresh parsley, basil and thyme and French dressing to taste. Season with salt and pepper and toss the ingredients together. Serve immediately or cover and chill in the refrigerator before serving.

1 Soak and cook the bulgur wheat according to the package instructions. Drain thoroughly and put into a serving bowl.

2 Meanwhile, cook the broad beans and petit pois in boiling water for 3 minutes. Drain and add to the prepared bulgur wheat.

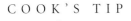

### COOK'S TIP
~
Use cooked couscous, boiled brown rice or wholewheat pasta in place of the bulgur wheat.

# Pappardelle and Provençal Sauce

*A classic French sauce of tomatoes and fresh vegetables adds colour and robust flavour to pasta.*

INGREDIENTS

*Serves 4*

2 small purple onions, peeled, root left intact

150 ml/¼ pint/⅔ cup vegetable stock

1–2 garlic cloves, crushed

60 ml/4 tbsp red wine

2 courgettes, cut into fingers

1 yellow pepper, seeded and sliced

400 g/14 oz can tomatoes

10 ml/2 tsp chopped fresh thyme

5 ml/1 tsp caster sugar

350 g/12 oz pappardelle

salt and freshly ground black pepper

fresh thyme and 6 black olives, stoned and roughly chopped, to garnish

3 Cook the pasta in a large pan of boiling salted water according to the instructions on the package, until tender. Drain the pasta thoroughly.

4 Transfer to a warmed serving dish and top with the vegetables. Garnish with fresh thyme and chopped black olives.

1 Cut each onion into eight wedges through the root end, to hold them together during cooking. Put into a saucepan with the stock and garlic. Bring to the boil, cover and simmer for 5 minutes, until tender.

2 Add the red wine, courgettes, yellow pepper, tomatoes, thyme and sugar. Season with salt and pepper. Bring to the boil and cook gently for 5–7 minutes, shaking the pan occasionally to coat the vegetables with the sauce. (Do not overcook the vegetables as they are much nicer if they are slightly crunchy.)

# Sweet and Sour Artichoke Salad

*Agrodolce is a sweet and sour sauce which works perfectly in this salad.*

INGREDIENTS

*Serves 4*

6 small globe artichokes

juice of 1 lemon

30 ml/2 tbsp olive oil

2 medium onions, roughly chopped

175 g/6 oz/1 cup fresh or frozen broad
 beans (shelled weight)

175 g/6 oz/1½ cups fresh or frozen peas
 (shelled weight)

salt and freshly ground black pepper

fresh mint leaves, to garnish

*For the salsa agrodolce*

120 ml/4 fl oz/½ cup white wine vinegar

15 ml/1 tbsp caster sugar

handful fresh mint leaves, roughly torn

1 Peel the outer leaves from the artichokes and cut into quarters. Place them in a bowl of water with the lemon juice.

2 Heat the oil in a large saucepan and cook the onions until golden. Add the beans and stir.

3 Drain the artichokes and add them to the pan. Pour in about 300 ml/½ pint/1¼ cups of water and cover. Simmer gently for 10–15 minutes.

4 Add the peas, season with salt and pepper and cook for a further 5 minutes, stirring from time to time, until the vegetables are tender.

5 Strain the vegetables through a sieve and place them in a bowl. Leave to cool, then cover and chill in the refrigerator.

6 To make the salsa, mix all the ingredients in a pan. Heat gently until the sugar has dissolved. Simmer for 5 minutes. Leave to cool. Drizzle over the salad. Garnish with mint leaves.

# Summer Tomato Pasta

*This is a deliciously light pasta dish, full of fresh flavours. Use buffalo-milk mozzarella if you can – the flavour is noticeably better.*

INGREDIENTS

*Serves 4*

275 g/10 oz/2¼ cups dried penne

450 g/1 lb plum tomatoes

275 g/10 oz mozzarella, drained

60 ml/4 tbsp olive oil

15 ml/1 tbsp balsamic vinegar

grated rind and juice of 1 lemon

15 fresh basil leaves, shredded

salt and freshly ground black pepper

fresh basil leaves, to garnish

3 Mix together the olive oil, balsamic vinegar, grated lemon rind, 15 ml/1 tbsp of the lemon juice and the basil. Season with salt and pepper. Add the tomatoes and mozzarella and leave to stand until the pasta is cooked.

4 Drain the pasta and toss with the tomato mixture. Serve immediately, garnished with fresh basil leaves.

1 Cook the pasta in boiling salted water, according to the package instructions, until just tender.

2 Quarter the tomatoes and remove the seeds, then chop the flesh into small cubes. Slice up the mozzarella into similarly sized pieces.

# Spanish Asparagus and Orange Salad

*Complicated salad dressings are rarely found in Spain – they simply rely on the wonderful flavour of a good quality olive oil.*

INGREDIENTS

*Serves 4*

225 g/8 oz asparagus, trimmed and cut
    into 5 cm/2 in pieces
2 large oranges
2 tomatoes, cut into eighths
50 g/2 oz romaine lettuce leaves, shredded
30 ml/2 tbsp olive oil
2.5 ml/½ tsp sherry vinegar
salt and freshly ground black pepper

1 Cook the asparagus in boiling salted water for 3–4 minutes, until just tender. Drain and refresh under cold water.

2 Grate the rind from half an orange and reserve. Peel both the oranges and cut into segments. Squeeze out the juice from the membrane and reserve the juice.

3 Put the asparagus, orange segments, tomatoes and lettuce into a salad bowl. Mix together the oil and vinegar and add 15 ml/1 tbsp of the reserved orange juice and 2.5 ml/1 tsp of the rind. Season the dressing with salt and pepper. Just before serving, pour the dressing over the salad and mix gently to coat.

COOK'S TIP
~
Cos or Little Gem lettuce can be used in place of romaine.

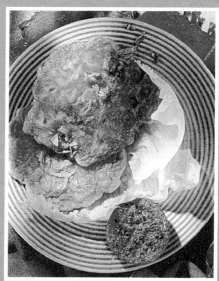

# LIGHT
# LUNCHES

# Grilled Goat's Cheese Salad

*Here is the salad and cheese course on one plate – or serve it as a quick and satisfying starter or light lunch. The fresh tangy flavour of goat's cheese contrasts with the mild salad leaves.*

INGREDIENTS

*Serves 4*

2 firm round whole goat's cheeses, such as
    Crottin de Chavignol (about
    65–115 g/2½–4 oz each)
4 slices French bread
olive oil, for drizzling
175 g/6 oz mixed salad leaves, including
    soft and bitter varieties
snipped fresh chives, to garnish

*For the dressing*
½ clove garlic
5 ml/1 tsp Dijon mustard
5 ml/1 tsp white wine vinegar
5 ml/1 tsp dry white wine
45 ml/3 tbsp olive oil
salt and freshly ground black pepper

1 To make the dressing, rub a large salad bowl with the cut side of the garlic clove. Combine the mustard, vinegar, wine, salt and pepper in a bowl. Whisk in the oil, 15 ml/1 tbsp at a time, to form a thick vinaigrette.

2 Cut the goat's cheeses in half crossways using a sharp knife.

3 Preheat the grill to hot. Arrange the bread slices on a baking sheet and toast on one side. Turn over and place a piece of cheese, cut side up, on each slice. Drizzle with oil and grill until the cheese is lightly browned.

4 Add the leaves and the dressing to the salad bowl and toss to coat the leaves thoroughly. Divide the salad among four plates, top each with a goat's cheese croûton and serve, garnished with chives.

# Broccoli and Cauliflower Gratin

Broccoli and cauliflower make an
attractive combination, and a
yogurt and cheesy sauce gives them
extra piquant flavour.

INGREDIENTS

Serves 4

1 small cauliflower (about 250 g/9 oz)

1 small head broccoli (about 250 g/9 oz)

150 g/5 oz/½ cup natural yogurt

75 g/3 oz/1 cup grated Cheddar cheese

5 ml/1 tsp wholegrain mustard

30 ml/2 tbsp wholemeal breadcrumbs

salt and freshly ground black pepper

1 Break the cauliflower and
broccoli into florets and cook
in lightly salted boiling water for
about 8–10 minutes, until just
tender. Drain well and transfer to
a flameproof dish.

2 Mix together the yogurt,
grated cheese and mustard,
then season the mixture with salt
and pepper and spoon over the
cauliflower and broccoli.

3 Preheat the grill to moderately
hot. Sprinkle the breadcrumbs
over the top of the vegetables and
grill until golden brown. Serve hot.

---

### COOK'S TIP

When preparing the cauliflower
and broccoli, discard the tougher
parts of the stalk, then break the
florets into even-size pieces so
they cook evenly.

# Tomato and Feta Cheese Salad

*Sweet sun-ripened tomatoes are rarely more delicious than when served with feta cheese and olive oil. This salad, popular in Greece and Turkey, is enjoyed as a light meal with pieces of crispy bread.*

*Serves 4*

900 g/2 lb tomatoes

200 g/7 oz feta cheese

120 ml/4 fl oz/½ cup olive oil, preferably
   Greek

12 black olives

4 sprigs of fresh basil

freshly ground black pepper

1 Remove the tough cores from the tomatoes with a small sharp knife.

### COOK'S TIP

Feta cheese has a strong flavour and can be salty. The least salty variety is imported from Greece and Turkey and is available from specialist delicatessens.

2 Slice the tomatoes thickly and arrange in a shallow dish.

3 Crumble the cheese over the tomatoes, sprinkle with olive oil, then strew with olives and fresh basil. Season with black pepper and serve at room temperature.

# Glazed Carrots with Cider

*This recipe is extremely simple to make. The carrots are cooked in the minimum of liquid to bring out the best of their flavour, and the cider adds a pleasant sharpness.*

INGREDIENTS

*Serves 4*

450 g/1 lb young carrots

25 g/1 oz/2 tbsp butter

15 ml/1 tbsp brown sugar

120 ml/4 fl oz/½ cup cider

60 ml/4 tbsp vegetable stock or water

1 tsp Dijon mustard

15 ml/1 tbsp finely chopped fresh parsley

1 Trim the tops and bottoms of the carrots. Peel or scrape them. Using a sharp knife, cut them into julienne strips.

COOK'S TIP

If the carrots are cooked before the liquid in the saucepan has reduced, transfer the carrots to a serving dish and rapidly boil the liquid until thick. Pour over the carrots and sprinkle with parsley.

2 Melt the butter in a frying pan, add the carrots and sauté for 4–5 minutes, stirring frequently. Sprinkle over the sugar and cook, stirring, for 1 minute or until the sugar has dissolved.

3 Add the cider and stock or water, bring to the boil and stir in the Dijon mustard. Partially cover the pan and simmer for 10–12 minutes, until the carrots are just tender. Remove the lid and continue cooking until the liquid has reduced to a thick sauce.

4 Remove the saucepan from the heat, stir in the chopped fresh parsley and then spoon into a warmed serving dish.

# Rocket, Pear and Parmesan Salad

*For a sophisticated start to an elaborate meal, try this simple salad of honey-rich pears, fresh Parmesan and aromatic leaves of rocket.*

*Serves 4*

3 ripe pears, Williams or Packhams
10 ml/2 tsp lemon juice
45 ml/3 tbsp hazelnut or walnut oil
115 g/4 oz rocket
75 g/3 oz Parmesan cheese
freshly ground black pepper
open-textured bread, to serve

1 Peel and core the pears and slice thickly. Moisten with lemon juice to keep the flesh white.

2 Combine the nut oil with the pears. Add the rocket leaves and toss.

3 Turn the salad out on to 4 small plates and top with shavings of Parmesan cheese. Season with freshly ground black pepper and serve with open-textured bread.

COOK'S TIP

If you are unable to buy rocket easily, you can grow your own from early spring to late summer.

# Tomato and Okra Stew

*Okra is an unusual and delicious vegetable. It releases a sticky sap when cooked, which helps to thicken the stew.*

*Serves 6*

15 ml/1 tbsp olive oil

1 onion, chopped

350 g/12 oz jar pimientos, drained

2 x 400 g/14 oz cans chopped tomatoes

275 g/10 oz okra

30 ml/2 tbsp chopped fresh parsley

salt and freshly ground black pepper

1 Heat the oil in a heavy-based pan. Add the onion and cook for 2–3 minutes.

2 Coarsely chop the pimientos and add to the onion. Add the chopped tomatoes and mix well.

3 Cut the tops off the okra and cut into halves or quarters if large. Add to the tomato sauce in the pan. Season with plenty of salt and pepper.

4 Bring the vegetable stew to the boil. Then lower the heat, cover the pan and simmer for 12 minutes, until the vegetables are tender and the sauce has thickened. Stir in the chopped parsley and serve at once.

# Tomato, Spring Onion and Coriander Salad

*Known as Cachumbar, this salad relish is most commonly served with Indian curries. There are many versions, and this one will leave your mouth feeling cool and fresh after a spicy meal.*

INGREDIENTS

*Serves 4*

3 ripe tomatoes

2 spring onions, chopped

1.5 ml/¼ tsp caster sugar

45 ml/3 tbsp chopped fresh coriander

salt

2 Halve the tomatoes, remove the seeds and dice the flesh.

3 Combine the tomatoes with the spring onions, sugar, chopped coriander and salt. Serve at room temperature.

1 Remove the tough cores from the tomatoes with a small sharp knife.

COOK'S TIP

This refreshing salad also makes a fine filler for pitta bread with hummus.

# Courgettes with Sun-dried Tomatoes

Sun-dried tomatoes have a concentrated, sweet flavour that goes well with courgettes.

### INGREDIENTS

*Serves 6*

10 sun-dried tomatoes, dry or preserved in oil and drained

175 ml/6 fl oz/¾ cup warm water

75 ml/5 tbsp olive oil

1 large onion, finely sliced

2 garlic cloves, finely chopped

1 kg/2¼ lb courgettes, cut into thin strips

salt and freshly ground black pepper

1 Slice the sun-dried tomatoes into thin strips. Place in a bowl with the warm water. Allow to stand for 20 minutes.

2 In a large frying pan or saucepan, heat the oil and stir in the onion. Cook over low to moderate heat until the onion softens but does not brown.

3 Stir in the garlic and courgette strips. Cook for about 5 minutes, continuing to stir the mixture.

4 Stir in the tomatoes and their soaking liquid. Season with salt and pepper. Raise the heat slightly and cook until the courgettes are just tender. Adjust seasoning and serve hot or cold.

# Artichoke Pasta Salad

*Broccoli and black olives add colour
to this delicious salad.*

*Serves 4*

105ml/7 tbsp olive oil

1 red pepper, quartered, seeded, and
thinly sliced

1 onion, halved and thinly sliced

5ml/1 tsp dried thyme

45ml/3 tbsp sherry vinegar

450g/1lb pasta shapes, such as penne
or fusilli

2 x 175g/6oz jars marinated artichoke
hearts, drained and thinly sliced

150g/5oz cooked broccoli, chopped

20–25 salt-cured black olives, stoned
and chopped

30ml/2 tbsp chopped fresh parsley

salt and ground black pepper

1 Heat 30ml/2 tbsp of the olive
oil in a non-stick frying pan.
Add the red pepper and onion
and cook over a low heat until just
soft, about 8–10 minutes, stirring
from time to time.

2 Stir in the thyme, 1.5ml/¼ tsp
salt and the vinegar. Cook,
stirring, for a further 30 seconds,
then set aside.

3 Cook the pasta in plenty of
boiling salted water according
to the instructions on the packet
until *al dente*. Drain, rinse with
hot water, then drain again.
Transfer to a large bowl. Add
30ml/2 tbsp of the oil and toss well
to coat thoroughly.

4 Add the artichokes, broccoli,
olives, parsley, onion mixture
and remaining oil to the pasta.
Season with salt and pepper. Stir to
blend. Leave to stand for at least
1 hour before serving or chill
overnight. Serve the salad at
room temperature.

# Green Lima Beans in Chilli Sauce

*Try this fabulous dish of lima beans
with a tomato and chilli sauce for
warming up on winter evenings.*

INGREDIENTS

*Serves 4*

450 g/1 lb green lima or broad beans,
    thawed if frozen

30 ml/2 tbsp olive oil

1 onion, finely chopped

2 garlic cloves, chopped

350 g/12 oz tomatoes, peeled, seeded
    and chopped

1 or 2 drained canned jalapeño chillies,
    seeded and chopped

salt

chopped fresh coriander, to garnish

1 Cook the beans in a saucepan
of boiling water for 15–20
minutes, until tender. Drain and
keep hot, to one side, in the
covered saucepan.

2 Heat the olive oil in a frying
pan and sauté the onion and
garlic until the onion is soft but
not brown. Add the tomatoes and
cook until the mixture thickens.

3 Add the jalapeños and cook for
1–2 minutes. Season with salt.

4 Pour the mixture over the
reserved beans and check that
they are hot. If not, return everything to the frying pan and cook
over low heat for just long enough
to heat through. Put into a
warmed serving dish, garnish with
coriander and serve.

# SIDE DISHES

~

# Runner Beans with Garlic

*Delicate and fresh-tasting flageolet beans and sautéed garlic add a distinctly French flavour to this simple side dish.*

### INGREDIENTS

*Serves 4*

225 g/8 oz/1¼ cups flageolet beans

15 ml/1 tbsp olive oil

25 g/1 oz/2 tbsp butter

1 onion, finely chopped

1–2 garlic cloves, crushed

3–4 tomatoes, peeled and chopped

350 g/12 oz runner beans, prepared
  and sliced

150 ml/¼ pint/⅔ cup white wine

150 ml/¼ pint/⅔ cup vegetable stock

30 ml/2 tbsp chopped fresh parsley

salt and freshly ground black pepper

1 Place the flageolet beans in a large saucepan of water, bring to the boil and simmer for ¾–1 hour, until tender.

2 Heat the olive oil and butter in a large frying pan and sauté the onion and garlic for 3–4 minutes, until soft.

3 Add the chopped tomatoes to the onions in the pan and continue cooking over a gentle heat, until they are soft.

4 Stir the flageolet beans into the onion and tomato mixture, then add the runner beans, wine, stock and a little salt. Stir. Cover and simmer for 5–10 minutes.

5 Increase the heat to reduce the liquid, then stir in the parsley, more salt, if necessary, and pepper.

# Puffy Creamed Potatoes

*This accompaniment consists of creamed potatoes incorporated into mini Yorkshire puddings. Serve them with a vegetable casserole or, for a meal on its own, serve two or three per person and accompany with salads.*

INGREDIENTS

*Makes 6*

275 g/10 oz potatoes

creamy milk and butter for mashing

5 ml/1 tsp chopped fresh parsley

5 ml/1 tsp chopped fresh tarragon

75 g/3 oz/⅔ cup plain flour

1 egg

about 120 ml/4 fl oz/½ cup milk

oil or sunflower margarine, for baking

salt and freshly ground black pepper

1 Boil the potatoes until tender and mash with a little milk and butter. Stir in the chopped parsley and tarragon and season with salt and pepper. Preheat the oven to 200°C/400°F/Gas 6.

2 Process the flour, egg, milk and a pinch of salt in a food processor or blender to make a smooth batter.

3 Place about 2.5 ml/½ tsp oil or a small knob of sunflower margarine in each of six ramekin dishes and place in the oven on a baking tray for 2–3 minutes, until the oil or fat is very hot.

4 Working quickly, pour a small amount of batter (about 20 ml/ 4 tsp) into each ramekin dish. Add a heaped tablespoon of mashed potatoes and then pour an equal amount of the remaining batter in each dish. Place in the oven and bake for 15–20 minutes, until the puddings are puffy and golden brown.

5 Using a palette knife, carefully ease the puddings out of the ramekin dishes and arrange on a large warm serving dish. Serve at once.

# Beetroot and Celeriac Gratin

*Beautiful ruby-red slices of beetroot and celeriac make a stunning light accompaniment to any main course dish.*

*Serves 6*

350 g/12 oz raw beetroot

350 g/12 oz raw celeriac

4 sprigs of fresh thyme, chopped

6 juniper berries, crushed

120 ml/4 fl oz/½ cup fresh orange juice

120 ml/4 fl oz/½ cup vegetable stock

salt and freshly ground black pepper

1 Preheat the oven to 190°C/375°F/Gas 5. Peel and slice the beetroot very finely. Quarter and peel the celeriac and slice very finely.

2 Fill a 25 cm/10 in diameter, cast iron, ovenproof or flame-proof frying pan with alternate layers of beetroot and celeriac slices, sprinkling with thyme, juniper and salt and pepper between each layer.

3 Mix the orange juice and stock together and pour over the gratin. Place over a medium heat and bring to the boil. Boil for 2 minutes.

4 Cover with foil and place in the oven for 15–20 minutes. Remove the foil and raise the oven temperature to 200°C/400°F/Gas 6. Cook for a further 10 minutes.

# Potatoes Dauphinois

*Rich, creamy and satisfying, this is a really comforting dish to serve when it's cold outside.*

INGREDIENTS

*Serves 4*

675 g/1½ lb potatoes, peeled and
   thinly sliced
1 garlic clove
25 g/1 oz/2 tbsp butter
300 ml/½ pint/1¼ cups single cream
50 ml/2 fl oz/¼ cup milk
salt and white pepper

1 Preheat the oven to 150°C/300°F/Gas 2. Place the potato slices in a bowl of cold water to remove the excess starch. Drain and pat dry with kitchen paper.

2 Cut the garlic in half and rub the cut side around the inside of a wide shallow ovenproof dish. Butter the dish generously. Blend the cream and milk in a jug.

3 Cover the base of the dish with a layer of potatoes. Dot a little butter over the potato layer, season with salt and pepper and then pour over a little of the cream and milk mixture.

4 Continue making layers, until all the ingredients have been used up, ending with a layer of cream. Bake in the oven for about 1¼ hours. If the dish browns too quickly, cover with a lid or with a piece of foil. The potatoes are ready when they are very soft and the top is golden brown.

# Red Cabbage in Port and Red Wine

*A sweet and sour, spicy red cabbage dish, with the added crunch of pears and walnuts.*

### INGREDIENTS

*Serves 6*

15 ml/1 tbsp walnut oil

1 onion, sliced

2 whole star anise

5 ml/1 tsp ground cinnamon

pinch of ground cloves

450 g/1 lb red cabbage, finely shredded

25 g/1 oz/2 tbsp dark brown sugar

45 ml/3 tbsp red wine vinegar

300 ml/½ pint/1¼ cups red wine

150 ml/¼ pint/⅔ cup port

2 pears, cut into 1 cm/½ in cubes

115 g/4 oz/½ cup raisins

115 g/4 oz/½ cup walnut halves

salt and freshly ground black pepper

1 Heat the oil in a large pan. Add the onion and cook gently for about 5 minutes, until softened.

COOK'S TIP

You can braise this dish in a low oven for up to 1½ hours.

2 Add the star anise, cinnamon, cloves and cabbage and cook for about 3 minutes more.

3 Stir in the sugar, vinegar, red wine and port. Cover the pan and simmer gently for 10 minutes, stirring occasionally.

4 Stir in the cubed pears and raisins and cook for a further 10 minutes, or until the cabbage is tender. Season with salt and pepper. Mix in the walnut halves and serve.

# Spicy Potatoes and Cauliflower

This dish is simplicity itself to make and can be eaten as a main meal with Indian breads or rice, a raita such as cucumber and yogurt, and a fresh mint relish.

### INGREDIENTS

*Serves 2*

225 g/8 oz potatoes

75 ml/5 tbsp peanut oil

5 ml/1 tsp ground cumin

5 ml/1 tsp ground coriander

1.5 ml/¼ tsp ground turmeric

1.5 ml/¼ tsp cayenne pepper

1 fresh green chilli, seeded and finely
   chopped

1 medium cauliflower, broken up into
   small florets

5 ml/1 tsp cumin seeds

2 garlic cloves, cut into shreds

15–30 ml/1–2 tbsp fresh coriander,
   finely chopped

salt

1 Cook the potatoes in their skins in boiling salted water for about 20 minutes, until just tender. Drain and let cool. When cool enough to handle, peel and cut into 2.5 cm/1 in cubes.

2 Heat 45 ml/3 tbsp of the oil in a frying pan or wok. When hot, add the ground cumin, coriander, turmeric, cayenne pepper and chilli. Let the spices sizzle for a few seconds.

3 Add the cauliflower and about 60 ml/4 tbsp water. Cook over medium heat, stirring continuously, for 6–8 minutes. Add the potatoes and stir-fry for 2–3 minutes. Season with salt, then remove from the heat.

4 Heat the remaining oil in a small frying pan. When hot, add the cumin seeds and garlic and cook until lightly browned. Pour the mixture over the vegetables. Sprinkle with the chopped coriander and serve at once.

# Peas with Baby Onions and Cream

*Ideally, use fresh peas and fresh baby onions. Frozen peas are an acceptable substitute if fresh ones aren't available, but frozen onions tend to be insipid and are not worth using. Alternatively, use the white parts of spring onions.*

## INGREDIENTS

*Serves 4*

175 g/6 oz baby onions

15 g/½ oz/1 tbsp butter

900 g/2 lb fresh peas (about 350 g/12 oz shelled or frozen)

150 ml/¼ pint/⅔ cup double cream

15 g/½ oz/2 tbsp plain flour

10 ml/2 tsp chopped fresh parsley

15–30 ml/1–2 tbsp lemon juice (optional)

salt and freshly ground black pepper

1 Peel the onions and halve them if necessary. Melt the butter in a flameproof casserole and fry the onions for 5–6 minutes over a moderate heat, until they begin to be flecked with brown.

2 Add the peas and stir-fry for a few minutes. Add 120 ml/ 4 fl oz/½ cup water and bring to the boil. Partially cover and simmer for about 10 minutes, until the peas and onions are tender. There should be a thin layer of water on the base of the pan – add a little more water if necessary or, if there is too much liquid, remove the lid and increase the heat until the liquid is reduced.

3 Using a small whisk, blend the cream with the flour. Remove the pan from the heat and stir in the combined cream and flour and chopped parsley. Season with salt and pepper.

4 Cook over a gentle heat for 3–4 minutes, until the sauce is thick. Taste and adjust the seasoning; add a little lemon juice to sharpen, if desired.

# Garlic Mashed Potatoes

*These creamy mashed potatoes have a wonderful aroma. Although two bulbs seems like a lot of garlic, the flavour is sweet and subtle when cooked in this way.*

*Serves 6–8*

2 garlic bulbs, separated into cloves, unpeeled

115 g/4 oz/½ cup unsalted butter

1.3 kg/3 lb baking potatoes

120–175 ml/4–6 fl oz/½–¾ cup milk

salt and white pepper

1 Bring a small saucepan of water to the boil over high heat. Add the garlic cloves and boil for 2 minutes, then drain and peel.

2 In a heavy frying pan, melt half of the butter over a low heat. Add the blanched garlic cloves, then cover and cook gently for 20–25 minutes, until very tender and just golden, shaking the pan and stirring occasionally. Do not allow the garlic to scorch or brown.

3 Remove the pan from the heat and cool slightly. Spoon the garlic and any butter from the pan into a blender or food processor fitted with a metal blade and process until smooth. Tip into a small bowl, press clear film on to the surface to prevent a skin forming and set aside.

4 Peel and quarter the potatoes, place in a large saucepan and add enough cold water to just cover them. Salt the water generously and bring to the boil over a high heat.

5 Cook the potatoes until tender, then drain and work through a food mill or press through a sieve back into the saucepan. Return the pan to a medium heat and, using a wooden spoon, stir the potatoes for 1–2 minutes to dry them out completely. Remove from the heat.

6 Warm the milk over a medium-high heat until bubbles form around the edge. Gradually beat the milk, remaining butter and reserved garlic purée into the potatoes, then season with salt, if needed, and white pepper.

# Frijoles

*A traditional Mexican bean dish that tastes great with tortillas and vegetable chilli.*

### INGREDIENTS

*Serves 6–8*

350 g/12 oz/1¼–1½ cups dried red kidney, pinto or black haricot beans, picked over and rinsed

2 onions, finely chopped

2 garlic cloves, chopped

1 bay leaf

1 or more small fresh green chillies

30 ml/2 tbsp corn oil

2 tomatoes, peeled, seeded and chopped

salt

sprigs of fresh bay leaves, to garnish

1 Put the beans into a pan and add cold water to cover by 2.5 cm/1 in.

2 Add half the onion, half the garlic, the bay leaf and the chilli or chillies. Bring to the boil and boil vigorously for about 10 minutes. Put the beans and liquid into an earthenware pot or large saucepan, cover and cook over low heat for 30 minutes. Add boiling water if the mixture starts to become dry.

3 When the beans begin to wrinkle, add 15 ml/1 tbsp of the corn oil and cook for a further 30 minutes, or until the beans are tender. Add salt to taste and cook for 30 minutes more, but try to avoid adding any more water.

4 Remove the beans from the heat. Heat the remaining oil in a small frying pan and sauté the remaining onion and garlic together until the onion is soft. Add the tomatoes and cook for a few minutes more.

5 Spoon 45 ml/3 tbsp of the beans out of the pot or pan and add them to the tomato mixture. Mash to a paste. Stir into the beans to thicken the liquid. Cook for just long enough to heat through, if necessary. Serve the beans in small bowls and garnish with fresh bay leaves.

# Roasted Potatoes, Peppers and Shallots

*This popular dish from North America's Deep South is often served in elegant New Orleans restaurants.*

INGREDIENTS

*Serves 4*

500 g/1¼ lb waxy potatoes

2 sweet yellow peppers

12 shallots

olive oil

2 sprigs of fresh rosemary

salt and freshly ground black pepper

1 Preheat the oven to 200°C/400°F/Gas 6. Wash the potatoes and blanch for 5 minutes in boiling water. Drain.

2 When the potatoes are cool enough to handle, skin them and halve lengthways. Cut each sweet yellow pepper lengthways into 8 strips, discarding the seeds and pith.

3 Peel the shallots and break them apart, allowing them to fall into their natural segments.

4 Oil a shallow ovenproof dish thoroughly with olive oil.

5 Arrange the potatoes and peppers in alternating rows and stud with the shallots.

6 Cut the rosemary sprigs into 5 cm/2 in lengths and tuck among the vegetables. Season the dish generously with olive oil, salt and pepper and bake in the oven, uncovered, for 30–40 minutes, until all the vegetables are tender.

# Deep-fried Root Vegetables with Spiced Salt

*All kinds of root vegetables may be finely sliced and deep-fried to make 'chips'. Serve as an accompaniment to an oriental-style meal or simply by themselves as a nibble.*

INGREDIENTS

*Serves 4–6*

1 carrot

2 parsnips

2 raw beetroot

1 sweet potato

peanut oil, for deep frying

1.5 ml/¼ tsp cayenne pepper

1 tsp sea salt flakes

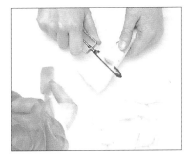

1 Peel all the vegetables, then slice the carrot and parsnips into long, thin ribbons, and the beetroot and sweet potato into thin rounds. Pat dry all the vegetables on kitchen paper.

### COOK'S TIP

To save time, you can slice the vegetables using a mandoline or a blender or food processor with a thin slicing disc attached.

2 Half-fill a wok with oil and heat to 180°C/350°F. Add the vegetable slices in batches and deep-fry for 2–3 minutes, until golden and crisp. Remove and drain on kitchen paper.

3 Place the cayenne pepper and sea salt in a mortar and grind together to a coarse powder.

4 Pile up the vegetable 'chips' on a serving plate and sprinkle over the spiced salt.

# Baked Sweet Potatoes

*Give sweet potatoes a Cajun flavour with salt, three different kinds of pepper and lavish quantities of butter. Serve half a potato per person as an accompaniment, or a whole one as a supper dish with a green salad peppered with watercress.*

Serves 3–6

3 pink-skinned sweet potatoes, about
    450 g/1 lb each
75 g/3 oz/6 tbsp butter, sliced
black, white and cayenne peppers
salt

1 Wash the potatoes and leave the skins wet. Rub salt into the skins, prick them all over with a fork and place on the middle shelf of the oven. Turn on the oven to 200°C/400°F/Gas 6 and bake for about an hour, until the flesh yields and feels soft when pressed.

2 The potatoes can either be served in halves or whole. For halves, split each one lengthways and make close criss-cross cuts in the flesh of each half. Then spread with slices of butter, and work the butter and seasonings roughly into the cuts with a knife point.

3 Alternatively, make an incision along the length of each potato if they are to be served whole. Open them slightly and put in butter slices along the length, seasoning with the peppers and a pinch of salt.

COOK'S TIP
~
Sweet potatoes cook more quickly than ordinary ones, and there is no need to preheat the oven.

# Fried Noodles, Beansprouts and Asparagus

*Soft fried noodles contrast beautifully with crisp beansprouts and asparagus in this super-quick recipe.*

*Serves 2*

115 g/4 oz dried egg noodles

60 ml/4 tbsp vegetable oil

1 small onion, chopped

2.5 cm/1 in piece of fresh root ginger, peeled and grated

2 garlic cloves, crushed

175 g/6 oz young asparagus spears, trimmed

115 g/4 oz beansprouts

4 spring onions, sliced

45 ml/3 tbsp soy sauce

salt and freshly ground black pepper

1 Bring a pan of salted water to the boil. Add the noodles and cook for 2–3 minutes, until just tender. Drain and toss in 30 ml/2 tbsp of the oil.

2 Heat the remaining oil in a wok or frying pan until very hot. Add the onion, ginger and garlic and stir-fry for 2–3 minutes. Add the asparagus and stir-fry for 2–3 minutes more.

3 Add the egg noodles and beansprouts and stir-fry for 2 minutes.

4 Stir in the spring onions and soy sauce. Season with salt and pepper, adding salt sparingly as the soy sauce will probably supply enough salt in itself. Stir-fry for 1 minute then serve at once.

# Rice with Seeds and Spices

*A change from plain boiled rice, and a colourful accompaniment to serve with spicy curries. Basmati rice gives the best texture and flavour, but you can use ordinary long grain rice instead, if you prefer.*

INGREDIENTS

*Serves 4*

5 ml/1 tsp sunflower oil

2.5 ml/½ tsp ground turmeric

6 cardamom pods, lightly crushed

5 ml/1 tsp coriander seeds, lightly crushed

1 garlic clove, crushed

200 g/7 oz/1 cup basmati rice

400 ml/14 fl oz/1⅔ cups vegetable stock

115 g/4 oz/½ cup natural yogurt

15 ml/1 tbsp toasted sunflower seeds

15 ml/1 tbsp toasted sesame seeds

salt and freshly ground black pepper

coriander leaves, to garnish

2 Add the rice and stock, bring to the boil, then cover and simmer for 15 minutes, or until just tender.

3 Stir in the yogurt and the toasted sunflower and sesame seeds. Season with salt and pepper and serve hot, garnished with coriander leaves.

1 Heat the oil in a non-stick frying pan and fry the spices and garlic for about 1 minute, stirring all the time.

### COOK'S TIP

Seeds are particularly rich in minerals, so they are a good addition to all kinds of dishes. Light toasting will improve their flavour.

# Parsnip and Chestnut Croquettes

*The distinctive sweet nutty taste of chestnuts blends perfectly with the similarly sweet but earthy flavour of parsnips. Fresh chestnuts need to be peeled but frozen chestnuts are easy to use and are nearly as good as fresh for this recipe.*

### INGREDIENTS

*Makes 10–12*

450 g/1 lb parsnips, cut roughly into small pieces

115 g/4 oz frozen chestnuts

25 g/1 oz/2 tbsp butter

1 garlic clove, crushed

15 ml/1 tbsp chopped fresh coriander

1 egg, beaten

40–50 g/1½–2 oz fresh white breadcrumbs

vegetable oil, for frying

salt and freshly ground black pepper

sprig of fresh coriander, to garnish

1 Place the parsnips in a saucepan with enough water to cover. Bring to the boil, cover and simmer for 15–20 minutes.

2 Place the frozen chestnuts in a pan of water, bring to the boil and simmer for 8–10 minutes. Drain, place in a bowl and mash roughly into a pulp.

3 Melt the butter in a saucepan and cook the garlic for 30 seconds. Drain the parsnips and mash with the garlic butter. Stir in the chestnuts and coriander. Season with salt and pepper.

4 Take about 15 ml/1 tbsp of the mixture at a time and form into small croquettes, about 7.5 cm/3 in long. Dip each croquette into the beaten egg and then roll in the breadcrumbs.

5 Heat a little oil in a frying pan and fry each of the croquettes for 3–4 minutes until crisp and golden, turning frequently so they brown evenly.

6 Drain the croquettes on sheets of kitchen paper, wiping away any excess oil, and serve at once, garnished with sprigs of fresh coriander.

# Red Fried Rice

*This vibrant rice dish owes its appeal as much to the bright colours of red onion, red pepper and tomatoes as it does to their flavours.*

INGREDIENTS

*Serves 2*

145 g/4½ oz/¾ cup basmati rice

30 ml/2 tbsp peanut oil

1 small red onion, chopped

1 red pepper, seeded and chopped

225 g/8 oz cherry tomatoes, halved

2 eggs, beaten

salt and freshly ground black pepper

1 Wash the rice several times under cold running water. Drain well. Bring a large pan of water to the boil. Add the rice and cook for 10–12 minutes.

2 Meanwhile, heat the oil in a wok until very hot. Add the onion and red pepper and stir-fry for 2–3 minutes. Add the cherry tomatoes and continue stir-frying for 2 minutes more.

3 Pour in the beaten eggs all at once. Cook for 30 seconds without stirring, then stir to break up the egg as it sets.

4 Drain the cooked rice thoroughly. Add to the wok and toss it over the heat with the vegetables and egg mixture for 3 minutes. Season with salt and pepper and serve immediately.

# Hot Parsnip Fritters on Baby Spinach

*Deep-frying brings out the luscious sweetness of parsnips, and their flavour is perfectly complemented by walnut-dressed baby spinach leaves.*

*Serves 4*

2 large parsnips

115 g/4 oz/1 cup plain flour

1 egg, separated

120 ml/4 fl oz/½ cup milk

115 g/4 oz baby spinach leaves, washed
 and dried

30 ml/2 tbsp olive oil

15 ml/1 tbsp walnut oil

15 ml/1 tbsp sherry vinegar

oil for deep frying

15 ml/1 tbsp coarsely chopped walnuts

salt, freshly ground black pepper
 and cayenne pepper

1 Peel the parsnips, bring to the boil in a pan of salted water and simmer for 10–15 minutes, until tender but not in the least mushy. Drain, cool and cut diagonally into slices about 5 cm/2 in long x 5 mm–1 cm/¼–½ in thick.

2 Put the flour in a bowl and make a well in the centre. Put the egg yolk in the well and mix in with a fork. Add the milk, while continuing to mix in the flour. Season with salt and black and cayenne peppers, and beat with a whisk until the batter is smooth.

3 Put the spinach leaves in a bowl. Mix the oils and vinegar. Season with salt and pepper.

4 When you are ready to serve, whisk the egg white to soft peaks, fold in a little of the yolk batter, then fold the white into the batter. Heat the oil for frying.

5 Shake the dressing vigorously, then toss the salad in the dressing. Arrange the leaves on 4 plates and scatter with walnuts.

6 Dip the parsnip slices in batter and fry until puffy and golden. Drain on kitchen paper and keep warm. Arrange the fritters on top of the salad leaves.

# Chinese Brussels Sprouts

*If you are bored with plain boiled Brussels sprouts, try pepping them up Chinese-style with this unusual stir-fried method.*

### INGREDIENTS

*Serves 4*

450 g/1 lb Brussels sprouts
5 ml/1 tsp sesame or sunflower oil
2 spring onions, sliced
2.5 ml/½ tsp Chinese five-spice powder
15 ml/1 tbsp light soy sauce

1 Trim the Brussels sprouts, then shred them finely using a large sharp knife or a food processor.

2 Heat the oil and add the sprouts and spring onions. Stir-fry for about 2 minutes, without allowing the mixture to brown.

3 Stir in the five-spice powder and soy sauce, then cook, stirring, for a further 2–3 minutes, until just tender. Serve hot with other Chinese dishes.

# Spinach with Raisins and Pine Nuts

*Raisins and pine nuts are perfect partners. Here, tossed with wilted spinach and croûtons their contrasting textures make a delicious main meal accompaniment.*

*Serves 4*

50 g/2 oz/⅓ cup raisins

1 thick slice crusty white bread

45 ml/3 tbsp olive oil

25 g/1 oz/⅓ cup pine nuts

500 g/1¼ lb young spinach,
   stalks removed

2 garlic cloves, crushed

salt and freshly ground black pepper

1 Put the raisins in a small bowl with boiling water and leave to soak for 10 minutes. Drain.

2 Cut the bread into cubes and discard the crusts. Heat 30 ml/2 tbsp of the oil and fry the bread until golden. Drain.

3 Heat the remaining oil in the pan. Fry the pine nuts until they are beginning to colour. Add the spinach and garlic and cook quickly, turning the spinach until it has just wilted.

4 Toss in the raisins and season with salt and pepper. Transfer to a warmed serving dish. Scatter with croûtons and serve hot.

VARIATION

Use Swiss chard or spinach beet instead of the spinach, and cook them a little longer.

# Festive Brussels Sprouts

*This recipe originated in France, where it is a popular side dish at Christmas time.*

INGREDIENTS

*Serves 4–6*

225 g/8 oz chestnuts

120 ml/4 fl oz/½ cup milk

500 g/1¼ lb/4 cups small tender
  Brussels sprouts

25 g/1 oz/2 tbsp butter

1 shallot, finely chopped

30-45 ml/2–3 tbsp dry white wine
  or water

1 Using a small knife, score a cross in the base of each chestnut. Bring a saucepan of water to the boil over medium-high heat, then drop in the chestnuts and boil for 6–8 minutes. Remove pan from the heat.

2 Using a slotted spoon, remove a few chestnuts from the pan, leaving the others immersed in the water until ready to peel. Before the chestnuts cool, remove the outer shell with a knife and then peel off the inner skin.

3 Rinse the pan, return the peeled chestnuts to it and add the milk. Top up with enough water to completely cover the chestnuts. Simmer over medium heat for 12–15 minutes until the chestnuts are just tender. Drain and set aside.

4 Remove any wilted or yellow leaves from the Brussels sprouts. Trim the root ends but leave intact or the leaves will separate. Using a small knife, score a cross in the base of each sprout so they cook evenly.

5 In a large, heavy frying pan, melt the butter over medium heat. Stir in the chopped shallot and cook for 1–2 minutes until just softened, then add the Brussels sprouts and wine or water. Cook, covered, over medium heat for 6–8 minutes, shaking the pan and stirring occasionally, adding a little more water if necessary.

6 Add the poached chestnuts and toss gently to combine, then cover and cook for 3–5 minutes more, until the chestnuts and Brussels sprouts are tender.

# Sweet and Sour Onions

*Cooked in this way, sweet baby onions make an unusual yet tasty side dish. This recipe originated in the Provence region of France.*

INGREDIENTS

*Serves 6*

450 g/1 lb baby onions, peeled

50 ml/2 fl oz/¼ cup wine vinegar

45 ml/3 tbsp olive oil

40 g/1½ oz/3 tbsp caster sugar

45 ml/3 tbsp tomato purée

1 bay leaf

2 sprigs of fresh parsley

65 g/2½ oz/½ cup raisins

salt and freshly ground black pepper

1 Put all the ingredients in a saucepan with 300 ml/ ½ pint/1¼ cups water. Bring to the boil and simmer gently, uncovered, for 45 minutes or until the onions are tender and most of the liquid has evaporated.

2 Remove the bay leaf and parsley, check the seasoning and transfer to a serving dish. Serve at room temperature.

# Szechuan Aubergine

*This medium-hot dish is also known as fish-fragrant aubergine in China, because the aubergine is cooked with flavourings that are often used with fish.*

INGREDIENTS

*Serves 4*

2 small aubergines

5 ml/1 tsp salt

3 dried red chillies

peanut oil, for deep frying

3–4 garlic cloves, finely chopped

1 cm/½ in piece of fresh root ginger, finely chopped

4 spring onions, cut into 2.5 cm/1 in lengths (white and green parts separated)

15 ml/1 tbsp Chinese rice wine or medium-dry sherry

15 ml/1 tbsp light soy sauce

5 ml/1 tsp sugar

1.5 ml/¼ tsp ground roasted Szechuan peppercorns

15 ml/1 tbsp Chinese rice vinegar

5 ml/1 tsp sesame oil

1 Trim the aubergines and cut into strips about 4 cm/1½ in wide and 7.5 cm/3 in long. Place the aubergine strips in a colander and sprinkle over the salt. Set aside for 30 minutes, then rinse thoroughly under cold running water. Pat dry with kitchen paper.

2 Meanwhile, soak the chillies in warm water for 15 minutes. Drain, then cut each chilli into four pieces, discarding the seeds.

3 Half-fill a wok with oil and heat to 180°C/350°F. Deep-fry the aubergine until golden brown. Drain on kitchen paper. Pour off most of the oil from the wok. Reheat the oil and add the garlic, ginger and white spring onion.

4 Stir-fry for 30 seconds. Add the aubergine and toss, then add the rice wine or sherry, soy sauce, sugar, ground peppercorns and rice vinegar. Stir-fry for 1–2 minutes. Sprinkle over the sesame oil and green spring onion and serve immediately.

# Chinese Greens with Soy Sauce

In this recipe, Chinese greens are prepared in a very simple way – stir-fried and served with soy sauce. The combination makes a very simple, quickly prepared, tasty accompaniment.

*Serves 3-4*

450 g/1 lb Chinese greens
30 ml/2 tbsp peanut oil
15–30 ml/1–2 tbsp plum sauce

2 Heat a wok until hot, add the oil and swirl it around.

3 Add the Chinese greens and stir-fry for 2–3 minutes, until the greens have wilted a little.

4 Add the plum sauce and continue to stir-fry for a few seconds more, until the greens are cooked but still slightly crisp. Serve immediately.

1 Trim the Chinese greens, removing any discoloured leaves and damaged stems. Tear into manageable pieces.

## VARIATION

You can replace the Chinese greens with Chinese flowering cabbage or Chinese broccoli, which is also known by its Cantonese name, choi sam. It has green leaves and tiny yellow flowers, which are also eaten along with the leaves and stalks. It is available at Asian markets.